Mass-Observation

The Mass-Observation Critical Series

The Mass-Observation Critical Series pairs innovative interdisciplinary scholarship with rich archival materials from the original Mass-Observation movement and the current Mass Observation Project. Launched in 1937, the Mass-Observation movement aimed to study the everyday life of ordinary Britons. The Mass Observation Project continues to document and archive the everyday lives, thoughts and attitudes of ordinary Britons to this day. Mass-Observation, as a whole, is an innovative research organization, a social movement and an archival project that spans much of the twentieth and early twenty-first centuries.

The series makes Mass-Observation's rich primary sources accessible to a wide range of academics and students across multiple disciplines, as well as to the general reading public. Books in the series include re-issues of important original Mass-Observation publications, edited and introduced by leading scholars in the field, and thematically oriented anthologies of Mass-Observation material. The series also facilitates cutting-edge research by established and new scholars using Mass-Observation resources to present fresh perspectives on everyday life, popular culture and politics, visual culture, emotions and other relevant topics.

Series Editors:

Jennifer J. Purcell is Professor of History at Saint Michael's College in Vermont, USA. Using Mass-Observation diaries and directives, her first book, *Domestic Soldiers* (2010), seeks to understand the day-to-day lives of six women on the home front during the Second World War. She is also the author of *Mother of the BBC: Mabel Constanduros and the Development of Light Entertainment on the BBC, 1925–1957* (Bloomsbury, 2020).

Benjamin Jones is Lecturer in Modern British History at the University of East Anglia in Norwich, UK. He is the author of The Working Class in Mid-Twentieth-Century England (2012), which was positively reviewed in Sociology, American Historical Review, Journal of Modern History, Journal of British Studies, The Historical Journal, Economic History Review, Contemporary British History, Twentieth Century British History and Planning Perspectives.

Editorial Board:
Fiona Courage, Head of Special Collections, University of Sussex in Brighton, UK
Lucy Curzon, Associate Professor of Contemporary and Modern Art History, University of Alabama, USA
Claire Langhamer, Director of the Institute of Historical Research, School of Advanced Study, University of London
Jeremy MacClancy, Professor of Anthropology, Oxford Brookes University, UK
Kimberly Mair, Associate Professor of Sociology, University of Lethbridge, Canada
Rebecca Searle, Lecturer in the Humanities, University of Brighton, UK
Matthew Taunton, Lecturer in the School of Literature, Drama and Creative Writing, University of East Anglia, UK

Published Titles:
The Biopolitics of Care in Second World War Britain, Kimberly Mair (2022)
Mass Observers Making Meaning, James Hinton (2022)
Mass-Observation, edited by Jennifer J. Purcell (2023)

Mass-Observation

Text, Context and Analysis of the Pioneering Pamphlet and Movement

Charles Madge and Tom Harrisson

***

Edited by Jennifer J. Purcell

BLOOMSBURY ACADEMIC
LONDON • NEW YORK • OXFORD • NEW DELHI • SYDNEY

BLOOMSBURY ACADEMIC
Bloomsbury Publishing Plc
50 Bedford Square, London, WC1B 3DP, UK
1385 Broadway, New York, NY 10018, USA
29 Earlsfort Terrace, Dublin 2, Ireland

BLOOMSBURY, BLOOMSBURY ACADEMIC and the Diana logo are
trademarks of Bloomsbury Publishing Plc

First published in Great Britain 2022
Published in partnership with the Mass Observation Archive

Copyright © Jennifer J. Purcell, 2022

Jennifer J. Purcell has asserted their right under the Copyright, Designs and
Patents Act, 1988, to be identified as Editor of this work.

Cover image: circa 1940; Young evacuees, wearing identification labels, prepare to travel.
(© Fox Photos/Getty Images)

All rights reserved. No part of this publication may be reproduced or
transmitted in any form or by any means, electronic or mechanical, including
photocopying, recording, or any information storage or retrieval system,
without prior permission in writing from the publishers.

Bloomsbury Publishing Plc does not have any control over, or responsibility for,
any third-party websites referred to or in this book. All internet addresses given
in this book were correct at the time of going to press. The author and publisher
regret any inconvenience caused if addresses have changed or sites have ceased
to exist, but can accept no responsibility for any such changes.

Every effort has been made to trace the copyright holders and obtain permission
to reproduce the copyright material. Please do get in touch with any enquiries or
any information relating to such material or the rights holder. We would be
pleased to rectify any omissions in subsequent editions of this publication
should they be drawn to our attention.

A catalogue record for this book is available from the British Library.

A catalog record for this book is available from the Library of Congress.

ISBN:	HB:	978-1-3502-2646-3
	PB:	978-1-3502-2647-0
	ePDF:	978-1-3502-2648-7
	ePUB:	978-1-3502-2649-4

Typeset by Integra Software Services Pvt. Ltd.

To find out more about our authors and books visit www.bloomsbury.com
and sign up for our newsletters.

Contents

List of illustrations	viii
List of contributors	ix
List of chronology	x
Introduction *Jennifer J. Purcell*	1
1 'The Observation by Everyone of Everyone': The project of Mass-Observation in 1937 *Ben Highmore*	7
2 Mass-Observation	29
3 Uncivilizing sociology: How Mass Observation can free the discipline *Rachel Hurdley*	69
4 Voices from the archive *Jennifer J. Purcell*	99
Bibliography	136
Index	141

Illustrations

1. Drawing of dresser, ca. 1938. Worktown Collection, Observations in Bolton. SxMOA 1/5/18/57/B/3. University of Sussex Special Collections: Mass Observation Archive.   73
2. 'Children play on wasteland near Gray St.' Humphrey Spender 1938. © Bolton Council. From the collection of Bolton Museum.   78
3, 4 and 5   Three photos of Slee Mantelpieces. Credit: Richard Slee: Mantelpiece Observations exhibition, Bolton Museum, 2020. Photo by Joel Fildes. © Bolton Council. From the collection of Bolton Museum.   81
6. Jimmy Floyd, Pigeon Crees, *c*. 1938 Ashington Group. By kind permission of the Ashington Group Trustees.   83
7. 'Washing day near Snowden St. Park Mill is visible in the background.' Humphrey Spender 1938. © Bolton Council. From the collection of Bolton Museum.   86
8. June 1937 Day Survey Mantelpiece Reports, D. Nicholson, Schoolboys' Reports. SxMOA 1/3/7/3: University of Sussex Special Collections: Mass Observation Archive.   88
9. C1154, Autumn 1983 directive SxMOA 2/1/13/1/4. University of Sussex Special Collections: Mass Observation Archive.   88

Contributors

Ben Highmore teaches Cultural Studies at the University of Sussex, UK. He has recently published work on Brutalism (*The Art of Brutalism: Rescuing Hope from Catastrophe in 1950s Britain*, Yale University Press, 2017) and feelings (*Cultural Feelings: Mood, Mediation, and Cultural Politics*, Routledge, 2017). He is currently finishing a book on post-war English taste in relation to the new middle classes and beginning another on the history of playgrounds. Previous books include *The Great Indoors: At Home in the Modern British House* (Profile Books, 2014) and *Ordinary Lives: Studies in the Everyday* (Routledge, 2011).

Rachel Hurdley is a research fellow in cultural sociology at Cardiff University School of Social Sciences, UK. Her research interests include qualitative methods and methodology, the meaning of home, memory work, materiality and archives. She is currently working on a book, *The Hidden History of the House* examining how domestic material forms, such as staircases and doors, are social, cultural and political productions. In 2013, she published *Home, Materiality, Memory and Belonging: Keeping Culture* (Palgrave MacMillan, 2013).

Jennifer J. Purcell is Professor of History at Saint Michael's College in Vermont, USA and co-editor of the Mass Observation Critical Series. She recently published *Mother of the BBC: Mabel Constanduros and the Development of Popular Entertainment on the BBC, 1925–1957* (Bloomsbury Academic, 2020). Drawing on Mass Observation diaries and directives, she published *Domestic Soldiers: Six Women's Lives in the Second World War* (Constable, 2010). Her current project, with Director of the Mass Observation Archive, Fiona Courage, considers Mass Observation and the Royalty for the Mass Observation Critical Series.

Chronology

1934	Charles Madge employed with *Daily Mirror*
Aug/Sept 1936	Tom Harrisson arrives in Bolton to start Worktown project
2 Jan 1937	*New Statesman* publishes Madge's letter calling for volunteers for 'an anthropology of our own people'
11 Jan 1937	Publication of *Savage Civilisation*
30 Jan 1937	'Anthropology at Home' letter, *New Statesman*. Madge, Harrisson, and Jennings announce Mass-Observation
Feb 1937	Day Surveys begin
June 1937	Publication of *Mass-Observation* (Muller)
Aug 1937	Publication begins of *M-O Bulletin*
Sept 1937	Publication of *May the Twelfth* (Faber & Faber)
Late-1937	Humphrey Jennings leaves the project
Mar 1938	Publication of *First Year's Work* (Lindsay Drummond)
Aug 1938	Worktown project in Bolton replaced by 'Social Factors in Economics' project, led by Madge; Harrisson takes over National Panel in London
Dec 1938	End of Day Surveys
Jan 1939	Directives begin
Jan 1939	Publication of *Britain by Mass-Observation* (Penguin)
Aug 1939	Diaries begin
3 Sept 1939	Second World War begins (Britain)
1940	Publication of *War Begins at Home* (Chatto and Windus)
1940	Madge creates and conducts social surveys for John Maynard Keynes

3 Feb 1940	First issue of *US*, Mass-Observation's Weekly Intelligence Service
17 May 1940	Last Issue of *US*
July 1940	Madge leaves Mass-Observation
Aug 1941	Publication of *Clothes Rationing Survey* (Advertising Services Guild, A.S.G.)
Fall 1941	Publication of *Home Propaganda* (A.S.G.)
Dec 1941	Publication of *A Savings Survey* (Working Class) (Rumble, Crowther, and Nicholas)
1942	Publication of *People in Production: Enquiry into British War Production* (Penguin)
April 1942	Publication of *People in Production* (John Murray for A.S.G.)
July 1942	Harrisson conscripted; Bob Willcock becomes acting director of Mass-Observation
1943	Publication of *War Factory* (Gollancz)
Jan 1943	Publication of *The Pub and the People: A Worktown Study by Mass-Observation* (Gollancz)
Mar 1943	Publication of *People's Homes* (John Murray for A.S.G.)
1944	Harrisson sent to Borneo as Major in the SOE; Bob Willcock takes over M-O in Harrisson's absence
May 1944	Publication of *Journey Home* (John Murray for A.S.G.)
1945	Publication of *Britain and Her Birth-rate* (John Murray for A.S.G.)
May 1945	End of war in Europe
Aug 1945	End of war in Japan
Sept 1946	Harrisson returns to UK
1947	Harrisson becomes curator of Sarawak Museum
1947	Publication of *Browns and Chester: Portrait of a Shop, 1780–1946* (Lindsay Drummond)

1947	Publication of *Puzzled People: A Study in Popular Attitudes to Religion, Ethics, Progress and Politics in a London Borough* (Gollancz)
April 1947	Publication of *Exmoor Village* (Harrup)
June 1947	Publication of *Peace and the Public* (Longman)
May 1948	Willcock leaves Mass-Observation, taking job with the Government Social Survey
June 1948	Len England becomes acting director of Mass-Observation
1949	M-O becomes limited company, focused on commercial market research
1949	Publication of *Report on Juvenile Delinquency* (Falcon)
1949	Publication of *People and Paint* (I.C.I.)
1949	Publication of *The Press and Its Readers* (Art and Technics)
Nov 1949	Publication of *Meet Yourself at the Doctor* (Naldrett)
Nov 1949	Publication of *Meet Yourself on Sunday* (Naldrett)
1950	Publication of *Voter's Choice: A Mass-Observation Report on the General Election of 1950* (Art and Technics)
1950	Madge becomes Professor of Sociology at Birmingham University
Nov 1955	Last Directive
1961	Publication of *Britain Revisited* (Gollancz)
1966	Publication of *Long to Reign over Us? The Status of the Royal Family in the Sixties* (William Kimber)
June 1967	Last Observer Diary
1969	Asa Briggs negotiates to bring MO material to Sussex University
1969	Publication of Angus Calder's *People's War* using MO material
Oct 1975	Archive opens to researchers

Jan 1976	Harrisson killed in road accident
1976	Publication of *Living through the Blitz* (Collins)
1977	Publication of Paul Addison's *Road to 1945* using MO material
1981	David Pocock and Dorothy Sheridan begin renewed Mass Observation Project (MOP)

Note: Mass-Observation with the hyphen refers to the mid-20th century project, while Mass Observation without the hyphen is a change made in the 2000s to make keyword searching easier. It tends to refer to the later project (1981–today) or to both projects together.

Introduction

Jennifer J. Purcell

In January 1937, amateur ornithologist/social explorer Tom Harrisson and poet/journalist Charles Madge penned the opening two chapters of *Mass-Observation*.[1] In these chapters, they outlined their view of the state of modern British society and the need for the woman- and man-in-the-street to become Observers of themselves and others in order to engage more fully with the world around them and to formulate and articulate their needs and desires on their own terms. The new organization they envisioned, and introduced in this volume, Mass-Observation, would provide a forum for the collection of these observations. Madge and Harrisson promised that the data collected from these Observers would be offered freely to scientific analysis and study, unfettered by narrow theoretical organization, open to multiple viewpoints and disciplines, closed off to no one. In sketching out this 'anthropology of ourselves', the authors hoped to combat the rising tide of superstition in the modern age and disarm 'The foisting on the mass of ideals or ideas developed by men apart from it ... [which] causes mass misery, intellectual despair and an international shambles'.[2]

There is a certain resonance reading *Mass-Observation* in 2022, eighty-five years after its publication. It is a resonance that once seemed theoretical and abstract, yet has become more tangible and meaningful since 2016. That year saw the Brexit referendum and an election that brought to the American presidency a corrupt real estate mogul who was unapologetic in sowing division, amplifying fears and courting conspiracies, and marked the rising tide of nationalisms and fascisms across the globe. The post-war Western European consensus that hoped European integration and cooperation would secure peace against another global war, and provide a bulwark against Russian aggressions, was unravelling. Those who understood the meaning of total war, whose living memory was seared with images and experiences of that devastation and who understood the importance of European cooperation, even if problematic and incomplete, become fewer and fewer with each passing year. Without that generation reminding us of the realities of world war, Europeans and Americans have become increasingly apathetic and forgetful, increasingly combative and resistant to compromise. As I write, Russia is invading Ukraine: the lead up to which has eerily (perhaps intentionally[3]) brought to mind the context of the late-1930s.[4]

Mass-media, while becoming more democratic with the advent of the internet and social media, has created silos that fracture civil discourse and allow hate groups, conspiracy theorists, racists, fascists and the like, a platform to recruit beyond their wildest imaginations in the days when recruitment relied on home-grown publications, word of mouth and postal communications. And while these online platforms feel democratic, in fact, state actors, politicians and media outlets manipulate them, and the more traditional media of television and radio, fuelling conspiracies and misinformation for financial gain, power or in covert acts of aggression against enemies.

Science and technologies move at a break-neck speed: offering the chance to connect, collaborate, entertain, learn, control and wage war in ways hard to imagine even ten years ago. Where once it took the expansive resources of nations, now individual billionaires invest phenomenal sums of money into private space programs; meanwhile, in these affluent nations that gave rise to such private wealth, poverty stalks in the shadows and middle classes teeter precariously on the edge of sustained employment and good health – the loss of either spelling certain economic disaster for these families. #MeToo and Black Lives Matter (BLM) movements have seismically unsettled the smug and entitled bastions of maleness and whiteness. Militaries rely on technologies that remove soldiers from the battlefield, digitizing death and making war feel like a video game to those who pull the trigger. Mobile phones track our movements, and the spectre of dystopian state control in authoritarian regimes, as well as in ostensibly democratic ones, grows darker as ever-sophisticated facial-recognition technologies emerge. Global warming threatens our future.

The uncertainties and lockdowns of Covid-19, including the politicization of masking and vaccination, communications technologies that have enabled remote working and learning, as well as the staggering potentialities of mRNA vaccination technology, only serve to underscore the mental effects and experiences of the culmination of the forces of technology, mass-media, deepening conflict, conspiracies and suspicions which seem so strikingly familiar in *Mass-Observation*.

Eighty-five years ago, Madge and Harrisson described the feeling of powerlessness that many felt in the face of new technologies and pointed to 'new methods of persuasion' developed by 'technical experts' for use in media, politics and advertising.[5] As a journalist reporting on the Wallis Simpson affair, Madge had inside knowledge into the ways in which editors and newspapers manufactured and manipulated public opinion.[6] That the authors of *Mass-Observation* wrote in the wake of the Abdication Crisis, which broke in December 1936, is made apparent in the heading on the first page of chapter one, 'The King wants to marry Mrs. Simpson: Cabinet says "No"'. A month earlier, the spectacular blaze that destroyed the Crystal Palace took on a particular significance to Mass-Observer David Gascoyne.[7] Historian of Mass Observation James Hinton writes, 'The destruction of two such icons of British identity within hardly more than a week could, Madge believed, hardly fail to stir up hidden depths in the national psyche and lay open to challenge the disempowering assumptions and superstitions (like those surrounding kingship) that held the masses in thrall.'[8]

Reading *Mass-Observation*, the frame of feeling broadens out, and the view encompasses a multitude of contexts: the Depression and mass unemployment sit alongside rapid scientific discoveries, the newness of radio and television, mass literacy and popular psychology. One month before the Crystal Palace blaze, 200 unemployed workers arrived in London after a 25-day, 300-mile peaceful march from the economically devastated Tyneside town of Jarrow, to deliver a petition to Parliament asking for the Government to revive industry in their town.[9] Ominous stirrings of war and conflict also fill the frame: the Cable Street Riot, which saw anti-fascists grapple with police and the British Union of Fascists under the leadership of Sir Oswald Mosley in the streets of London, erupted on 4 October 1936. Earlier that year, German forces tested the mettle of the treaty of Locarno signatories, who vowed to stop any attempt to remilitarize the Rhineland, and found it wanting. Mussolini's Italian forces invaded Ethiopia (Abyssinia) in October 1935. Far-right groups stormed the French Chamber of Deputies in February 1934, instigating political and civil unrest that historian Julian Jackson argues 'marked the beginning of a French civil war' that lasted over a decade, until the fall of German occupation in 1944.[10] Civil war erupted in Austria for a few violent months in 1934 and the Spanish Civil War, which broke out in early 1936, continued to rage as Mass-Observation's first publication hit the newsstands.

This is the first re-issue of *Mass-Observation* since its publication eighty-five years ago, and as part of the Mass Observation Critical Series, the volume includes essays which consider the moment of that publication and imagine the potential futures of the continuing project, which was restarted in 1981. When the authors penned *Mass-Observation*, they imagined intersections with diverse disciplines, such as sociology, psychology and anthropology. The diverse collection of materials collected by Mass-Observation since 1937 is of great value to cultural studies and has deeply engaged social, cultural and art historians alike. The essays in this volume speak to this diverse range of interest, if only as a starting point. Indeed, the purpose of the *Mass Observation Critical Series* is to demonstrate the continued value and still as yet unrealized potential of the original Mass Observation Project (1937–55) and the ongoing Mass Observation Project (MOP, 1981–today) for both academic and popular audiences across a wide range of disciplines.[11] Essays, interviews and new interpretations of published Mass Observation material hint at the immense possibilities that still lie untapped within the archive, as well as the potential for future MOP directives and community projects, and opportunities to expand and diversify the MOP panel.

Reminding us of the anxieties and uncertainties embedded in the political, social and cultural contexts of 1937, Ben Highmore's essay serves as an introduction to the original text and deeply considers the expressed aspirations of the author-founders of *Mass-Observation* as an 'emergent project': 'future-oriented, in-process, reflexive, unfinished and malleable'. He argues that the 1937 pamphlet was a call to raise collective consciousness in the fight against the rising wave of Nazism and Fascism, civil and imperial conflicts, and the machinations of populist leaders, politicians, media outlets and marketing managers to manipulate public opinion and behaviour, all of which threatened the fabric of everyday life and practices. Pointing to the 'transformation of consciousness' resulting from Observers' acts of self-reflection and social observation, Highmore underscores the symbiotic relationship between Observers on the one hand, and Mass-Observation and researchers on the other. Studying directive responses, one can witnesses this process at work: many Observers unpack their observations, thoughts and feelings on the page, thus 'expand[ing] the consciousness of the observer', while simultaneously opening a window into the interiority of Observers.

When Madge and Harrisson proposed this project in *Mass-Observation*, they hoped to collect and preserve such observations, imagining that such work could benefit future researchers and contribute to 'an increase in the general social consciousness'.[12] It is through this process of 'collective consciousness raising' that Highmore argues 'holds out the promise of a truly democratic form of anti-fascism' and the promise of a civil project that can unsettle and disrupt the power of mass media, big business and political actors.

Rachel Hurdley's essay considers how this democratization at the centre of Mass-Observation's vision and methodologies might present a 'compelling future for sociology as a politicised, public endeavour of active citizens and engaged academics'. Her essay explores the multimodal approaches of the organization as potential disruptors of accepted research and analytical methods of contemporary sociological inquiry. Her reflections on the practices and experiences of archival research are particularly insightful as they encourage us to pay attention to absence and presence in our research and writing, the sustained dialogue between researcher and observer, the politics of knowledge creation and selection of material, as well as the shifting potentials and possibilities of physical and digitized archival material.

If Hurdley's essay reminds us of the shifting possibilities of different forms of archival experiences and inquiry, the interviews in the final chapter further underscore the magic and messiness of the early archive at the University of Sussex before it was fully catalogued or digitized. In these interviews with long-time Director and Archivist of the Mass Observation Archive, Dorothy Sheridan, and two early researchers, Nick Stanley and Penny Summerfield, a history emerges of the archive at Sussex and its centrality in debates regarding subjectivity and the value of personal narratives across disciplines. The interviews also provide insight into the beginnings of the Mass Observation Project and its operation from the 1980s to today, signalling potential challenges and pathways into the future for Mass Observation.

Given the heightened fears and anxieties that press in upon us today, and the deep cynicism of our own age, it seems admirable that a group of individuals imagined a democratic civil project aimed at taking down power brokers, confronting fascists and coming to grips with the forces of technology. For all of the criticism that the founders and the organization have faced over the years, it is useful to remember that, at least in this initial pamphlet, the authors welcomed dialogue and criticism. And it is worth remembering that the 'emergent project' of Mass Observation continues to offer possibilities for democratic initiative and power. Reading *Mass-Observation* in 2022 reminds one that there is still so much that might be done: imagine, for instance, the power that engaging more and more diverse Observers into the project and expanding beyond England, and the UK, might bring to bear on these forces that continue to threaten civil society from outside and from within.

Notes

1. Nick Hubble, *Mass Observation and Everyday Life: Culture, History, Theory* (Basingstoke: Palgrave Macmillan, 2006), 111.
2. Tom Harrisson, Humphrey Jennings & Charles Madge, 'Anthropology at Home', *New Statesman and Nation*, January, 30 1937, 155.
3. The invasion took place less than a week after the fifty-eighth annual Munich Security Conference wrapped up proceedings. Russian allegations regarding Eastern Ukraine are strikingly similar to German allegations regarding the Sudetenland of Czechoslovakia, which ultimately resulted in the Munich conference in September and October 1938.
4. This introduction was penned in February 2022. As the manuscript is prepared for publication in June 2022, the war in Ukraine continues to rage.
5. *Mass-Observation* this volume, 39.
6. James Hinton, *The Mass Observers: A History, 1937–1949* (Oxford: OUP, 2013), 7.
7. Ben Highmore, 'The Observation by Everyone of Everyone: The Project of Mass-Observation in 1937', this volume, 7–28.
8. Hinton, *The Mass Observers*, 7.
9. For an excellent account of the march, see David Clay Large, *Between Two Fires: Europe's Path in the 1930s* (New York: W. W. Norton, 1990), 180–222.
10. Julian Jackson, *France: The Dark Years, 1940–1944* (Oxford: OUP, 2001), 65.
11. *Mass-Observation Critical Essays*, ed. Lucy Curzon and Ben Jones, for this series will demonstrate the wide disciplinary appeal of Mass Observation.
12. *Mass-Observation*, this volume, 45.

1

'The Observation by Everyone of Everyone': The project of Mass-Observation in 1937

Ben Highmore

Mass-Observation intends to make use not only of the trained scientific observer, but of the untrained observer, the man in the street. Ideally, it is the observation by everyone of everyone, including themselves.[1]

Introduction

The republication of the original *Mass-Observation* pamphlet from 1937 is an opportunity to consider Mass-Observation (henceforth MO) not as a historical institution that was particularly active in the 1930s and 1940s, nor as a sociological practice from the mid-century that was then picked up again in the 1980s, but as an emergent project. The word 'project' here refers to practices that are future-oriented, in-process, reflexive, unfinished and malleable.[2] To see MO as an emergent project requires less hindsight (and less concern with the clashing personalities and positionalities of its founders) and more attention to the plans and promises as they are announced in a set of inaugural public statements of which the pamphlet is the lodestone. The pamphlet is a text addressed to an audience written under the collective authorship of MO (even if the individual details of that authorship were made evident within the text). It is the result of an outpouring of energy, primarily from two young men, Charles Madge and Tom Harrisson, in the first few months of 1937 (January to April).[3] It is a quasi-manifesto, but it is also a dossier of cultural experiments, intellectual resources and a list of aligned projects.

In what follows, I pay attention to the specificity of the statements that MO issued in the first half of 1937 and examine the form that they took and the way that they addressed their audience. These are statements that are simultaneously practical and reflexive: they are proposals for material activities and experiments in observing; they also consider questions of epistemology, the historical moment of the project, the hubris of the title 'civilization', and how an 'anthropology of ourselves'[4] connects with the broad landscape of science and art. Paying attention to the materiality of their public statements means noticing, for instance, the insistent repetition of the physical address of MO: 6 Grote's Buildings, London, S.E.3. This was the address of Charles Madge and his wife the poet and scholar Kathleen Raine, and their children: it was also MO headquarters for correspondence and filing. The address is written out three times in the pamphlet alone. It is included in nearly all the articles, essays and letters that were published under the name of Mass-Observation or Charles Madge at this time.[5] When talking about MO's address to its audience we need to take the literalism of the term 'address' seriously: a public was being addressed (written or spoken to) and at the same time it was being given an address (to write to) so as to constitute itself as a public body of Mass Observers. The statements being made were recruiting statements, invitations to participate. MO, then, was an experiment in producing civil society, building a public sphere, or a counter public sphere.

The project of Mass-Observation, as it appeared in the early months of 1937 to people reading various announcements in weekly magazines such as the *New Statesman and Nation* or newspapers like *News Chronicle*, or paying the one shilling for the *Mass-Observation* pamphlet,[6] or coming across articles in *New Verse* or *Left Review*, was a rallying call to a participatory 'science' of the everyday, to co-create a collective 'poem' of amassed observations, and to join forces with anthropologists, psychologists and sociologists. (The scare quotes around 'science' and 'poem' are there precisely because these are the terms that require most elucidation in the context of the *Mass-Observation* pamphlet.) The social function of MO, as articulated in early 1937, was, I'm going to argue, *consciousness raising* in the face of the rise of a murderous atavism evident at the time in Germany, Spain and in the Italian presence in Ethiopia (referred to as Abyssinia in the pamphlet). To argue this, I'm going to outline MO's explanation for its existence and to examine the methods of participation it was imagining (only some of which were realized). I will conclude by stepping out of the 1937 moment and looking briefly at the influence of this experimental project of participatory consciousness raising, and its pertinence for democratic culture today.

Science and superstition

The project of a collective observation of daily life might be an idea that could occur at any point in modern history. The conditions that suggest that we don't really know what others think, feel, believe and do, could be a general condition of mass, class-based, regionally distinct, society.[7] The fact that this idea occurs with such force and momentum at the end of 1936 suggests that the MO project had a distinct political and social urgency.[8] The first explanation of this urgency was the sense of everyday life being, potentially, annulled or at least drastically altered. The rise of fascism in Germany, Spain and Italy (and its obvious expansionist appetite as evidenced by Mussolini's treatment of Ethiopia) is the catastrophe that MO faces: 'we are all in danger of extinction from such outbursts of atavism'.[9] The study of everyday life emerges at a point where forms of routine life are in danger of disappearing.[10] This is the deep context of MO and it is what throws light on other events that surround the beginnings of the project. For instance, MO were particularly fascinated by the destruction of the Crystal Palace and the way its demise caught the popular imagination. This building, dubbed 'the People's Palace', had once been the centrepiece of the 1851 *Great Exhibition of the Works of Industry of All Nations*, but had been moved from its original site and re-erected in the London suburbs to host tea dances and dog shows. On the night of November 29, 1936, and continuing into the morning of the next day, it burnt to the ground while thousands of people came out to watch.[11] The poet David Gascoyne, who saw the massive glow of the fire when he was returning home from an MO meeting at 6 Grote's Building, recalls:

> For most of us, – we Mass-Observationists that is to say, – it represented in a sort of symbolic way an image of world-conflagration which we were already beginning to think of as about to break out, and we felt that it meant this, unconsciously, to the general public, hence the unusual fascination it seemed to have for everyone at the time.[12]

The sense of a looming catastrophe being (both literally and symbolically) 'in the air' is part of the anxious, febrile atmosphere that surrounds MO.

For MO, then, the everyday life of a population isn't simply the habits and routines that continue day-in, day-out; it is also the way that this ordinary life is the host for all sorts of feelings and affects, symbols and metaphors. The threat of war intensified a general realization: so-called civilized mass society isn't founded on rationality, knowledge and functionality. From the perspective of MO, and informed by their interests in anthropology, psychology and evolutionary biology as well as surrealism, everyday life is orchestrated as much by anxieties, superstitions, ambitions, hopes and neuroses as it is by anything approaching deliberative logic. Everyday life is simultaneously rational and irrational, and this seems as true of a tribal community in Borneo as a so-called civilized country like Britain. Such a science of everyday life couldn't simply amass 'facts' about eating habits and work routines, it would also need to attend to superstitions, myths, feelings and fantasies. Sometimes the superstitions would seem merely quaint or odd, at other times superstition was another name for murderous bigotries like genocidal racism: 'the revival of racial superstition' is how MO represent the situation in Germany in 1937.[13]

The second explanation for MO's emergence in 1937 relates to the way myths and superstitions could be mobilized and amplified by new social techniques and technologies. In one sense 'mass-society' is only constituted through forms of mass-communication and accompanying mass-literacy. The landscape of newspapers, advertising hoardings, radio and television (then in its experimental infancy) constitutes part of the social formation that MO are responding to. Mass-media and their various enchantments, of which advertising was a crucial force, perform a number of social functions: they usually address an imagined and abstract social subject, unified by a purported allegiance to nation, or to quality tobacco, or to cleanliness.[14] MO set out from a recognition that the fields of entertainment, advertising, newspapers and magazines work to entangle a population with superstitions:

> In 1937, the advertising agencies and daily newspapers employ the best empirical anthropologists and psychologists of the country. These great organisations base their work on the assumption that the human mind is suggestible and they aim their suggestions at that part of the human mind in which the superstitious elements predominate.[15]

The word 'superstition' has a similar semantic function as the word 'myth' has in anthropology, or the word 'ideology' in political theory. Yet what MO are not proposing is a form of ideology critique aimed at unmasking the class interests at work in various belief systems (for instance), nor are they proposing a functionalist analysis of how myth operates across a society.[16] MO's view on superstition is, I think, unsettled. On the one hand it seems inconceivable for a society to operate outside of superstition. Reading *Mass-Observation* there is the sense that there is something inevitably human about superstitions. But it is also clear that the superstitiousness of human beings is being exploited by advertisers, newspapers and entertainment industries, and that there exists the potential and actual deployment of superstitiousness by fascism. But if a society based on deliberative logic is not possible, what is to be done about superstition? Here I think we begin to see a set of strategies that are being established not to erase superstition but to open it up to conscious reflection:

> The first practical measure to be aimed at would seem to be the mobilisation of observers on a mass basis to carry out according to an agreed programme the observation of the habits of different classes, and their concealed wishes as they reveal them in their superstitions, fantasies and fears, and as they are exploited by advertisements, by newspapers and films.[17]

Writing about how this might work in the context of the 1936 Constitutional Crisis which resulted in the Abdication of Edward VIII in December, Madge invokes Freud to suggest that ancient social taboos (such as killing a king) are unconsciously understood, and that a mass observation of superstitions would 'lay bare the sources of this influence' and 'would have the effect of lessening the magical power' of the monarchy.[18] The critique of superstition and the denuding of its power would be performed intuitively by a mass attention to such aspects of social life.

Other strategies are employed that suggest that MO was imagining itself as a counter public sphere. National daily newspapers, for instance, speak on behalf of a nation with a singular voice: thus, a newspaper might declare that Britain at one moment feels anger and at another moment dishonour or sorrow, and so on, where that national subject is the addressee of the newspaper (in other words, a newspaper is telling its readers what and how they should feel). Mass-media performed its own irrationalism, encouraging rumour and anxiety, revelling in the magic properties of new commodities and conjuring myths about detergents, food stuffs and political figures. Against this landscape, the 'mass' of Mass-Observation is meant to register differently. If the mass of mass-media is characterized by its ability to de-differentiate, to homogenize, as it communicates from the one to the many, the mass of Mass-Observation is all about registering a sea of differences. For MO the civil population is treated as ontologically heterogeneous and eccentric, as well as epistemologically opaque.

The question of difference is a keen one for discussions of democracy. How can a form of governance respond to the needs of the many, when that many is diverse, heterogeneous and difficult to know outside the blunt instrument of national census data or the piecemeal accounts by sociologists seeking answers to specific questions? The position of representative democracy means that the interests of large and powerful minorities are often catered for at the expense of a multitude of difference. One way of improving democracy might be to make that unknown hinterland of a population known. This is I think the nearest that MO come to having a 'politics' that could be named as such. It is true that one of the founders (Charles Madge) was a member of the communist party and that the other was involved in Liberal politics (Tom Harrisson), but I think these personal commitments are not easily extractable from the statements that MO make at this time. For instance, in his essay 'Magic and Materialism', which was published at the same time as the pamphlet, Madge can write:

> As a Marxist, I have drawn Marxist implications from the work it [MO] sets out to do, but it is left to any individual member of the group to draw his own implications. My statement is therefore a personal one, with which some members of the group may agree, but which is not binding for all. Our common front is the application of materialism to superstition.[19]

And here 'materialism' signals a commitment to intellectual approaches grounded in empiricism (psychology, evolutionary biology, anthropology and so on) as well as looser empirical projects such as reportage, documentary films and experiments in observational poetry.

The word 'science' is used throughout the pamphlet, and it is clear that MO were absolutely dedicated to declaring the project as 'scientific'; MO 'aims to be a scientific study of human social behaviour'.[20] But what is less clear is what they meant exactly by that term. The words 'science' and 'scientific' perform various functions in the pamphlet. One of its primary tasks is to further emphasize that the project is a materialist approach to social phenomena and one not governed by politics. In this way 'science' is a way of making it clear that MO belong to a form of enquiry that tests out hypotheses by relying on extensive evidence, and is not motivated by political or moral positions: 'It is the task of science not to pass a moral judgment on superstition, but simply to examine and describe it, leaving to others to decide whether they want it or not.'[21] This refusal of moral and political positioning is what the word science offered them, and was a way of addressing and recruiting participants where permissiveness was taken for granted: 'there is no criminal and all human beings are of equal interest'.[22] But 'science' is not an unalloyed good in these pages. If 'superstition' lies on one side, and 'science' or 'materialism' lies on the other, then there is an aspect of the practice of science that seems more likely to feed the world where superstitions roam – a world of fear and anxiety, of lust and ambition. This is another use of science, not to understand human life but to throw it into jeopardy by using science to produce industrial forms of killing. Foremost in the mind of MO was the idea of a poison gas that was unseen, deadly and with indiscriminate targets. This is where science intensifies the existential anxiety that we as a species tend to fill with myths and superstitions: 'we look to science to help us, only to find that science is too busy forging new weapons of destruction to give heed to our questions'.[23] So, for MO the use of the term science was far from simple: it established some allegiances within science (testing via evidence, abstaining from *a priori* political or moral assessment) while also distancing itself from other modes of being scientific (what we might now call the 'military-industrial-complex'): more crucially and ambitiously MO sought to contribute to 'a new epoch of science'.[24] It is worth noting how MO publications use the authorial voices of established scientists (both from the social sciences and the natural sciences) to underwrite their work. In the pamphlet it is the zoologist Julian Huxley and in the publication *First Year's Work 1937-38* it is the anthropologist Bronislaw Malinowski. And yet MO's vision of science can be seen as decidedly at odds with the 'official' line on science. This is evident in Huxley's forward where he puts forward the eugenic position that science should be used to control populations, and it is evident in Malinowski's absolute refusal to see any overlap between science and poetry. This establishes a clear tension between the 'parent' culture of Malinowski and Huxley and the young pretenders of science – Madge, Harrisson and others aligned with MO. We can get a much better sense of what underpins young pretender science, and what sort of scientific outlook it was, by following some of its underlying principles as well as the practices it was imagining and encouraging in 1937.

A methodology of description

Ten months after the publication of the pamphlet, MO were able to reflect on a year's worth of work. In their publication *First Year's Work 1937-38*, they begin with an account of 'Smoking as a Social Habit', which starts with an epigraph from David Hume's *Treatise on Human Nature*, which was first published in 1739-40. It is worth quoting it again here:

> We must therefore glean up our experiments in this science (i.e., the Science of Man) from a cautious observation of human life, and take them as they appear in the common course of the world, by men's behaviour in company, in affairs and in their pleasures. Where experiments of this kind are judiciously collected

and compared, we may hope to establish on them a science which will not be inferior in certainty, and will be much superior in utility, to any other of human comprehension.[25]

This quote comes from the end of the introduction to Hume's extraordinary book. By using this quote as an epigraph for their work, MO are alerting us to their indebtedness to Hume's conception of humanism as a form of experimental science. Indeed, Hume's philosophy is based on a methodology that resonates across the project of MO: 'the only foundation we can give to this science itself must be laid on experience and observation.'[26]

In *Treatise on Human Nature* Hume is arguing against a philosophy that begins with arguments and logics which are then applied to life, and for a philosophy that starts from actual sensate, sensorial life. It is worth spending a paragraph or two drawing out the relevance of Hume for MO. David Hume was the leading voice in what became known as the Scottish Enlightenment, and his philosophical attitude resonates either directly or indirectly across the humanities and social sciences in the Anglophone world. Hume's *Treatise* is a sustained defence of radical empiricism and its attendant method of experimentation. It argues that human beings are first and foremost governed by their passions – by pride, jealousies, hunger, humility, desires, fellow-feelings and so on – and that abstract principles are always scaffolded on top of these passions. It is not hard to see how this position might coalesce with MO's understanding of the importance of superstition, and how rational arguments might be less important than a world of feelings and attitudes. What was crucial to MO was that they weren't simply involved in collecting 'opinions' but were actively directed to ways of uncovering unconscious desires animating the popular imagination.[27]

Hume subtitled the *Treatise* as 'An Attempt to introduce the experimental Method of Reasoning'. The experiments that Hume conducted were observational and today we would refer to them as a form of auto-ethnography. He is his own primary empirical subject: he notices, for instance, how different the world appears to him when he is disconsolate compared to when he is ebullient. He notices that his subjectivity only reconciles itself as a singular (centripetal) entity when he feels pride or humility, while the other passions produce a much more diffuse and centrifugal form of selfhood. As a form of empiricism he argues simultaneously that the observing subject is inconsistent (his or her observations might vary depending on their mood, for instance), and that this inconsistency is not detrimental to their observing but is actually a sign of the sensitivity of the observing apparatus (the human subject). It is our ability to be affected – hurt, saddened, delighted – that make us responsive and nuanced instruments of observation. Our sensitivities and sentiments make us both inconsistent and capable of the most finely tuned observations.

You can see Hume's influence across all of MO's practice. The sense of a responsive subjectivity that alters depending on its context is a decisive element in the endeavour to find out what and how people feel and believe. For instance, Tom Harrisson writing about the difficulty of ascertaining the landscape of public opinion recognizes that attitudes and thoughts might alter depending on the context where an opinion is voiced (a well-known issue for opinion researchers). Yet for Harrisson there are also inconsistencies at the level of the subject (between conscious and unconscious self):

> Here, we are concerned mainly with what people say; within this we must distinguish:
> What a person says to a stranger.
> What a person says to an acquaintance.
> What a person says to a friend.
> What a person says to his wife.
> What a person says to himself.
> What a person says in his sleep.
> It is at the level of wife, self and dream that the most significant, as well as the most difficult, assessment of opinion can be made.[28]

The inconsistency of the human subject for gathering information becomes even more problematic when MO thinks about the mass of observers that they are going to recruit.

> In science the ideal observer is as objective as a machine. But when it comes to dealing with human behaviour, even the scientist finds it impossible to rule out his own subjective bias. With our untrained Observers we must expect this to be even more marked. Feelings will interfere in the choice of facts and method of approach, especially through the unconscious omission of certain facts.[29]

If we follow Hume here, an experimental science of human behaviour (which might be a fairly exact way of characterizing MO in its inaugural moment) requires observers whose feelings not only interfere with observation but through this interference offers them the capacity to register and respond to crucial elements of everyday life. MO uses the metaphor of weather to describe the role of the untrained observers: 'They will be the meteorological stations from whose reports a weather-map of popular feeling can be compiled.'[30] It is an apt metaphor for capturing something of the responsive capacities of observers.

We should note that it is 'popular feeling' that is the object here, and that the metaphor posits two dynamic inconsistencies: the volatility of weather fronts and air pressure, and the plasticity of the barometer so that it can sensitively register changing pressures, temperatures and such like. It is the sensitivity of the barometer (its ability to be affected) that establishes the quality of its readings.

While the voluntary Mass-Observer required no training prior to joining MO, they did receive a form of training when they joined, and elements of this are outlined in the pamphlet. In the training there seems to be a tension in terms of what it might consist of and what values it pursues. At one point it is suggested that the goal is 'objectivity': 'the first task of an Observer is to write an objective report on himself'.[31] But this seems to have less to do with an observing subject disengaging their emotions (for instance) and more about giving a fuller account of themselves including their class background, etc. Objective, here, can mean something like describing aspects that you might think of as 'taken-for-granted', or that 'goes without saying', as well as those that wouldn't show you in an ideal light. Objectivity in this sense is an invitation to refuse the twin lures of a narcissistic ego and social probity.

The more extended descriptions of training have much less to do with a putative objectivity, and more to do with expanding the imaginative capacities and sensitivities of the observer. One of the training techniques that MO suggests requires responding to a set of images. MO means something more than 'picture' by the term 'image': 'The image, in our sense, is something between an idea and a sensation.'[32] The example that they offer is 'a house with broken windows'. One way of describing such an image is that it is 'charged' (emotionally, affectively) while also being undecided. For instance, a picture of a house with broken windows might suggest a romantic ruin, a crumbling family home or something less slowly entropic and more malign: a house after a bomb attack from the air, a house attacked by snipers, the target of vandalism, etc. Observers would use these image cards and respond to a series of prompts to describe them, to find patterns across the images, to link them to historical moments and so on. The cards were intended to 'sharpen the powers of observation' but also to 'strengthen the imagination':

> Pictures play a continual part in our lives, though often unrealised. We intend to issue a series of images, like packs of playing cards, and to suggest various exercises which can be played with them. These exercises will be designed to sharpen the powers of observation of a particular type – the observation of images […] these exercises will strengthen the imagination.[33]

What would strengthening the imagination mean here apart from becoming more responsive to the 'sensational' aspects of the image and of everyday life by an increased sensitivity towards charged phenomena?

We can see the way that an 'interference of feeling' is seen as a positive attribute in the practice of observation in a short observational account that is used in two MO texts to exemplify both the ordinariness of the observational reports and their richness. This is an example of an observation in response to a direction to report on 'examples of the behaviour of superiors to subordinates and vice versa'. The woman's account is one of thirty-six she provided:

> *Coming home on a Midland Red 'Bus from Birmingham (a distance of approx. 6 miles) I was sitting on the front seat, near the large sliding door. There was a cold easterly wind blowing in my eyes, I touched the Conductor on the sleeve to attract his attention, and said 'May we have the door closed, Conductor?' He turned round and leant towards me in a confidential way, and then said in a most insolent manner 'Yes, when I'm ready to shut it!' I was too surprised to make any reply. The door remained open until I left the 'bus.*[34]

What makes this a compelling account for MO is the way it registers everyday feelings of what subordination feels like. It isn't an objective account, if by that is meant something stripped of emotional involvement, but something ripe with passional energies. Indeed one way of reading the text is as an orchestration of attractions and affects: the leaning in of the conductor in his 'confidential' (and seemingly intimate) way doubles the hurt caused by the 'insolent manner' in which he seems to scorn her and belittle her. We can feel her reel back 'too surprised to make a reply' and the continued hurt as the wind kept blowing into the bus and into her eyes. This isn't testimony that could be simply true or false. But it is a social fact of feeling. If we'd been on the bus you or I might have viewed the event differently. Was the woman being overly haughty and patronising, was the conductor merely using the tiny power bestowed on him to regain some dignity out of the exchange? Was the belittling, if that is what it was, a form of misogyny? These are not questions that the testimony can answer: but what it can answer is 'what do everyday forms of belittlement feel like and what do they look like when they appear?', and here the 'interference of feeling' is exactly what is required to answer that question. For Charles Madge the subjectivity of the woman's response is an objective account of feeling as a social fact: 'Such observations as the insolent or "confidential" manner of the 'bus conductor, though subjective, become objective because the subjectivity of the observer is one of the facts under observation.'[35]

In an interesting shift in the ground of MO's articulation of their scientific approach, testimony such as this account of a supercilious bus conductor is simultaneously scientific and poetic. For Madge this account 'is (i) scientific, (ii) human, and therefore, by implication, (iii) poetic'.[36] The mediating term here is 'human', and it is this mediation that allows MO to name the experimental method as scientific, and to understand poetics as the outcome of this 'new' science (which can also be understood as an older Human science, newly collectivized). To name the mass data gathering that MO wanted to undertake in 1937 as a new form of poetry or poetics requires some clarification. To say that science equals poetry when you mediate it via humanism is not a straightforward claim. For one thing it would register quite differently as a method for recruiting participants: to be asked to participate in a scientific endeavour as a social good is quite different from being asked to participate in a collective form of poetry. Yet it is worth sticking with MO here and trying to figure out what they meant by 'poetic'. I think we get a hint about the relationship between poetics and science when MO discusses the books they intend to produce. They state that there will be three main kinds of publications: the first would be 'collective books' with titles such as 'What is on your mantelpiece?'; the second would be 'cheap editions of scientific works'; and the third would be a monthly bulletin that would be an 'experiment in co-operative newspaper-making'.[37] The books that MO went on to produce didn't stick to this division but the purest example we have of what they meant by 'collective books' was sent for publication in August 1937 – *May the Twelfth: Mass-Observation Day-Surveys 1937 (by over two hundred observers)*.[38] This is an arrangement of observations and newspaper reports that took place on 12 May 1937, which also happened to be the day of the Coronation of George VI.[39]

The *May the Twelfth* book is the one example of what we might today call a dataset. The book itself is an arrangement of observations and newspaper clippings with the minimal of editorial intervention. The reader is given various framing mechanisms for understanding the collection, for instance by learning about the scale and the range of observers:

> The Observers by this time cover the whole country. They are in the industrial centres, in rural and urban areas, in country towns, suburbs and villages. They include coalminers, factory hands, shopkeepers, salesmen, housewives, hospital nurses, bank clerks, business men, doctors and schoolmasters, scientists and technicians.[40]

One way of understanding this unusual book is by thinking of it as a giant cubist account of a historical event – history not just seen from 'below' but seen from every conceivable (and inconceivable) angle, including studious avoidance. The poetry here is both in the assemblage and also in the 'rawness' of the observational descriptions. This is volunteered ethnographic materials that haven't yet been digested, processed and synthesized. The social sciences might gather together similar 'informant' accounts, but in the conventional social science treatise the mass of utterances that might constitute an ethnographic archive are obscured and discarded to make way for the interpretation and the discovery of social patterns: with *May the Twelfth* there is little there but this mass of micro-ethnographies.

MO imagined time and again that this 'raw material' was the real contribution that they were making and that their interpretations of findings would always be secondary, and rarely an end to the matter. To name this material 'poetry' was a way of caring for it and de-instrumentalizing it. To be poetry was to be distinct from information: a poem couldn't be spent in the same way that a piece of information might be. And it was the fact that these raw nuggets of life were inexhaustible that was going to be key to their value and their longevity. It was as poems that they also held some autonomy: they weren't owned by MO and they weren't owned by the forms of interpretation that might come along and sort them and interpret them. The cubist refraction that they might have as edited together in a book by Jennings and Madge was just one iteration of the life that they could have (and should have). A hundred other arrangements could be imagined:

> The results that should be obtainable when the method is fully developed should be of interest to the social worker, the field anthropologist, the politician, the historian, the advertising agent, the realistic novelist and indeed any person who is concerned to know what people really want and think. We propose to hold our files open to any serious worker.[41]

The same materials then could be reworked from any number of perspectives. The day of the Coronation could be looked at from the perspective of someone interested in crowd behaviour, or someone keen to get a sense of the way that the monarchy were being thought about in different regions of England (which is the primary location of the observers, though some of the observations come from Scotland). It is the relative autonomy of these observations and their ability to be deployed in numerous accounts that give them the quality of poetry, and it is this that allows the observations to shift from data to a form of practice that can be thought of as consciousness raising.

Attitudes, feelings and consciousness raising

As an emergent project, Mass-Observation in 1937 doesn't have any explicit social aims beyond the attempt at a collective description of everyday life and social behaviour. As a project it didn't lack ambition, far from it, but that ambition didn't come with a programme of social improvement through specific acts of transformation (reforming local government, or introducing new practices of social care, for instance). Given that MO emerged at a moment where the very idea of a democratic and caring society was resting on a precipice it might seem odd that MO doesn't frame its project as a science that will provide answers to social problems such as class distinction, racism and debt. Yet if MO are unprepared to think of the observations as serving an instrumental purpose, it was also clear that observing wasn't a means to an end, wasn't merely the best way of collecting data. For MO there was something in the process of becoming an observer, something in the method of attending to daily life as an observer (or someone interested in these mass-observations) that could be claimed as a value for democracy, and as an orientation that might somehow inoculate a population against Nazism.

The way that MO framed the contribution that could be made by participating in the project was around the idea of consciousness and social consciousness. It is this which brings together their interest in superstition, media and materialism. The world of 1937 was a world of newspapers and radio. Ideas and opinions were circulating at a mass scale, coming into the home via live voices echoing from new domestic technologies, as well as disseminating through the much older media of print journalism. Such techniques have their effects and affects: 'Every day the social consciousness is modified by the news reported in the newspapers and on the wireless.'[42] If consciousness is being altered by mass-media it is not being altered by simply expanding the information that is circulating. A social consciousness can be altered by advertising, by gossip, by information about scientific discoveries, by unfounded fears circulating as truths, by creating heroes and villains, targets to despise and targets to envy. Media orchestrate social affects.

In the place of media, a practice of observation offers a delay in the continuum of experience. It requires consideration, evaluation, a practice of weighing-up. In a world where the continuum of experience includes a barrage of media (which today may seem laughably small) the very practice of observation and the attendant period of writing-up institutes a re-evaluation at a number of levels.

At the most immediate level it involves a re-evaluation of the self and activities routinely undertaken. As a 'working class girl' writes:

> Mass-Observation, it was something new, something to talk about; the things I do in the house are monotonous, but on the 12th, they are different somehow, letting the dog out, getting up, making the dinner, it makes them important when they have to be remembered and recorded. It is in the nature of scientific work, but not necessarily by experts, and I have an interest in science. It also widens my horizon; I had never really wondered what people had on their mantelpieces, and maybe these reasons are vague, but I like the work, it gives me a sense of importance, whether justified or not, I don't know.[43]

The activities of housework don't specifically change, but the perception of them (the consciousness of them) does. It is this transformation of consciousness that is at the heart of the MO project in its relation to the mass of voluntary observers. But it isn't a transformation of consciousness that is only available to the singular observer: observers are encouraged not only to participate by supplying their own testimony but to read the testimony of others in a way that would expand their sense of everyday life.

So, the practice of observation works on two levels at the same time. It expands the consciousness of the observer by making them alert to the materiality of their everyday lives (to 'counteract the tendency so universal in modern life to perform all our actions through sheer habit'), and it expands their social consciousness by reconfiguring their observation as one of many observations. The mass observers weren't recruited on the basis of individualism. The term 'scientific' is crucial here in guarding against an individualized and isolationist attitude towards observation: they were being asked to report on the world around them, to be a representative of more than themselves: as neighbours, as working men and women, as struggling teachers, as retired nurses. The attentiveness that MO were encouraging was one aimed not just at the self but at the environment: MO 'will encourage people to look more closely at their social environment than ever before and will place before them facts about other social environments of which they know little or nothing. This will effectively contribute to an increase in the general social consciousness'.[44]

It is the observation and the triangulation of observations that performs consciousness raising. On its own a singular observation is limited. It can increase thoughtfulness, reflection and evaluation, but it is as a *mass*-observer that the alteration of consciousness is performed as the raising of *social consciousness*, and it is this which is the main task of MO. Again 'science' has its role in insisting that observers saw themselves as part of a much larger formation where class experiences, for instance, could be triangulated across other testimonies, or where metropolitan experiences can be compared to rural occurrences. The social value of MO as an observation-gathering group is through the emphasis on mass participation. As Charles Madge writes the goal of MO is 'to raise the level of consciousness collectively of the whole mass'.[45] It is worth putting this quote into its full context. Madge is laying out the early promises of MO as a response to the preponderance of magic and superstition in modern society and he is imagining a new collective practice that is both an art practice and form of collective science. He is imagining a new way of working (which is of course MO):

> His observations must be mass-observations, his data mass-data. His works of art must satisfy not his own isolated fantasy, but the needs and wishes of the masses; his scientific generalisations must apply not only to himself but to every member of his society. His problem is not to raise to the level of his own consciousness aspects of humanity hitherto concealed or only guessed at, but he has to raise the level of consciousness collectively of the whole mass, he has to induce self-realisation on a mass scale.[46]

It is this collective consciousness raising rather than any political position as such, that is the key to understanding MO in 1937. It is this which holds out the promise of a truly democratic form of anti-fascism, one that couldn't be blinded by the light of the sort of mass-psychology of fascism where difference is extinguished in the name of 'race' or 'nation'. It is a collective consciousness that has a perspective of the mass rather than a leader of the mass (be that a charismatic leader, a belligerent newspaper editor, a canny marketing department or even a progressive social scientist). And it is this collective consciousness that is a democratic science, a science for all.

Science for all

When the *Mass-Observation* pamphlet was published in June 1937 it was widely reviewed by the press.[47] One immediate result of all this publicity was the increase in participants: 'Within a few weeks more than a thousand people had applied to be Observers and the number is steadily rising.'[48] But if MO were an attractive proposition for many, it was also a source of amusement and disdain for others. Sorting through the criticism that they received during their first year, and the specific responses that their pamphlet received, they list some of the names that they had been called: 'Mass-Mystics, spies, Nosey Parkers, Peeping Toms, lopers, doodlers, snoopers, envelope steamers.'[49] The willingness of people to participate in a project like MO might be understood as a continuation of an idea of civil and civic responsibility. Seen within a longer tradition of 'civic science', the MO project follows cultural practices of collective ornithology and natural history societies that recruited amateurs to pursue their mass observations from the mid-nineteenth century.[50] But what might be deemed community-minded and civic responsibility when it came to the world of birds or natural habitat could seem prurient or invasive when it was directed at the human species and its habitat, particularly in a country that lived under what MO described as 'the ultra-repressed conditions of our society'.[51] Seen from today's perspective we could say that one aspect of MO is a willingness to transform the public sphere into something that could incorporate material that was usually 'relegated' to the private sphere: feelings, desires, anxieties and so on.

In an age before the internet, the private sphere did have a public existence but one that was often regulated in terms of who got to speak and who got to be heard. Elaborate accounts of feelings and moods existed but was a preserve primarily of diarists and novelists who could garner publishing contracts – it was the preserve of a privileged class. In 1937 the limited amount of working-class literature that existed had little to say about what it felt like to undergo the routine drudgeries of housework. While the internet has certainly allowed anyone with access to share their experiences, there is no guarantee that these experiences are heard beyond a circle of intimates. The internet has clearly recalibrated our experience of a public sphere but the issue of who speaks and who is heard is as alive today as it was in 1937. Attempts to democratically alter this calibration in a way that fundamentally changes collective consciousness requires attending as much to the process of listening as speaking, and framing the work of speaking within a different understanding of what it means to speak in a public setting.

One scheme that directly relates to MO and carries this ethos of collective consciousness raising was a BBC television project from the 1990s called *Video Nation*. It was established in 1993 by Chris Mohr and Mandy Rose for the Community Programmes Unit and its impetus was to increase participation within television: 'The contributors were given their Hi-8 camera for one year, during which time they filmed their everyday lives. More than 10,000 tapes were shot and sent into the BBC, from which approximately 1,300 shorts were edited and shown on television, the first of which was *Mirror* by Gordon Hencher.'[52] *Mirror* consisted of an older man regarding himself in a mirror and reflecting on what it feels like to age, to become an old man. Other programmes consisted of people describing their post-natal depression, or their experiences of racist abuse. They were intimate disquisitions that seemed to be broadcast directly from someone's bedroom or kitchen to an audience of anywhere from 1 million to 9 million viewers. These micro-programmes continued for a decade at which point the project moved online. The producers of *Video Nation* visited the MO archive as part of their research for the project and came away with a strong sense that they were following in the wake of MO. Nico Carpentier has shown that while the move to online dissemination potentially allowed for a greater degree of participation it didn't increase its ability to democratize media representations of a diverse population.[53]

This chapter has paid close attention to the original problematic facing MO: how does a population become known to itself? This problematic is crucial if democracy is going to be more than a technique of political power and become part of a living culture. For the MO team the problematic is a condition of media. Put starkly; unless there are mechanisms for a population to represent itself as a day-to-day reality, then there are plenty of powerful forces prepared to speak in its name. Thus MO establishes itself as a counter-form to the way that radio and newspapers speak 'on behalf' of an audience or a readership. It is this which makes MO part of our contemporary world. But it is also relevant today because it suggests a form of participation, a form of self-disclosure that is in stark contrast to the forms of 'sharing' that are encouraged by social media. The insistence on 'science' within MO is again an insistence on the fact that the observer isn't a sovereign subject but is part of a collective. MO needs to be distinguished from, on the one hand, ethnographic projects that go out to solicit opinions to pursue specific social phenomena, on the other hand it also needs to be distinguished from the narcissistic address of so much social media. The mass observations of MO are singular without being individualist. It is the insistence on collective consciousness and the solicitation towards a civil project that speaks to us today as an antidote to our over individualistic society as well as to a society that is still beset by the monstrous shadow of fascism.

Notes

1   Mass-Observation, *Mass-Observation* [written by Charles Madge and Tom Harrisson] (London: Muller, 1937), this volume, 34–5.
2   Today MO exist as an archival repository that is continually being added to (at the Keep in Falmer, UK). It is organized as two distinct but connected bodies of work: one called

the Mass-Observation Archive (dealing with the material from 1930s, 1940s and 1950s); the other is called the Mass-Observation Project which is an on-going data collection that dates back to 1981. The reason that the later work is named a project is because it is still in operation, still open to change. By referring to the inaugural moment as a 'project' I'm attempting to capture something of the unfixed and experimental character of MO as it was emerging in 1937, to apprehend its historicity as an emergent practice.

3   James Hinton, *The Mass Observers: A History, 1937–1949* (Oxford: Oxford University Press, 2013), 1 puts the ages of the two as twenty-seven and twenty-six when they met in January 1937, but they were actually twenty-five and twenty-four (Harrisson, the slightly older of the two, was born September 26, 1911, Madge October 11, 1912).

4   Mass-Observation, *Mass-Observation*, this volume, 34.

5   By focusing on MO as a *public* formation in the first half of 1937 my account downplays the role of the Bolton (and Blackpool) ethnographic project. This aspect of MO, where the focus was less on mass collective observing and more on a selected band of observers, will come more to the fore with the publication of Mass-Observation, *First Year's Work 1937–38*, London: Lindsay Drummond, 1938.

6   Prior to decimalization in 1971 there were twenty shillings in the pound. A shilling was equivalent to five pence.

7   For the historian James Vernon the essential characteristic of modernity is its ability to create 'a new society of strangers' through massive population expansion and fragmentation, and forms of abstract, bureaucratic governance. In this regard modernity could be seen as the historical condition of possibility for MO. See James Vernon, *Distant Strangers: How Britain Became Modern* (Berkeley: University of California Press, 2014), 23.

8   While it is common to date the start of MO as January 1937, the literature of the time dates it as November 1936, before Tom Harrisson's participation. See the biographical note for Charles Madge in C. Day Lewis, ed., *The Mind in Chains: Socialism and the Cultural Revolution* (London: Frederick Muller, 1937), 146 where Madge 'founded, in November 1936, "Mass-Observation", an organization for studying behaviour and mentality by means of a mass of observers'.

9   Mass-Observation, *Mass-Observation*, this volume, 35.

10 Those studies most attuned to everyday life (anthropology and ethnology) are historically founded as a response to the threatened loss of traditional forms of everyday life within societies and social groups undergoing uninvited colonialization and modernization. The morbidity and melancholy at the heart of these sciences is explored by Michel de Certeau (with Dominique Julia and Jacques Revel) in 'The Beauty of the Dead: Nisard', in *Heterologies: Discourse of the Other*, trans. Brian Massumi (Minneapolis: University of Minnesota Press, 1986), 119–36.

11 Alison Edwards and Keith Wyncoll, *'The Crystal Palace Is on Fire!' Memories of the 30th November 1936* (London: The Crystal Palace Foundation 1986).

12 This is Gascoyne looking back on his diaries from the time. David Gascoyne, *Journal 1936–37, Death of an Explorer, Léon Chestov* (London: Enitharmon Press, 1980), 9.
13 Mass-Observation, *Mass-Observation*, this volume, 35. Anti-Semitism is a pressing concern for MO from the start and is one of the themes that they propose to investigate in the letter to *New Statesman and Nation* signed by Tom Harrisson, Charles Madge and Humphrey Jennings published on January 30, 1937. For an extended treatment of MO and race see Tony Kushner, *We Europeans? Mass-Observation, Race and British Identity in the Twentieth Century* (Aldershot: Ashgate, 2004).
14 MO's relationship to advertising and mass-media differed significantly from intellectual figures such as F. R. Leavis who, in the 1930s, warned about the ill effects of both. It was partly MO's partial allegiance to surrealism that allowed them to see advertising and newspapers as dream-like material that could be useful in revealing mass-desires (on this see my chapter on MO in *Everyday Life and Cultural Theory* [London: Routledge, 2002], particularly pp. 81–9). For the clearest account of Leavis's position on advertising, mass-media and mass-literacy see F. R. Leavis and Denys Thompson, *Culture and Environment* (London: Chatto & Windus, 1933). The secondary literature around mass-media and universal literacy is enormous, for a useful guide that connects across both Leavises (Queenie and F.R) and MO see Christopher Hilliard *To Exercise Our Talents: The Democratization of Writing in Britain* (Cambridge: Harvard University Press, 2006)
15 Mass-Observation, *Mass-Observation*, this volume, 39.
16 MO's familiarity with both ideology critique and functionalism in sociology and anthropology are shown in the dossier section of the pamphlet particularly section (g) 'Ground Plan for Research' and (h) 'Organisations with Similar Aims' – which starts out by naming the 'Institute for Social Research', which is another name for the Frankfurt School. See Mass-Observation, *Mass-Observation*, this volume, 64.
17 Charles Madge, 'Magic and Materialism', *Left Review*, no. 3 (1937): 33.
18 Madge, 'Magic and Materialism', 33.
19 Madge, 'Magic and Materialism', 34.
20 Mass-Observation, *Mass-Observation*, this volume, 34.
21 Mass-Observation, *Mass-Observation*, this volume, 35.
22 Mass-Observation, *Mass-Observation*, this volume, 45.
23 Mass-Observation, *Mass-Observation*, this volume, 35.
24 Mass-Observation, *Mass-Observation*, this volume, 35.
25 David Hume, *Treatise on Human Nature* (edition ed. L. A. Seby-Bigge) (Oxford: Clarendon Press, 1896), xxiii. Quoted in Mass-Observation, *First Year's Work 1937–38*, ed. Charles Madge and Tom Harrisson (London: Lindsay Drummond, 1938), 8. I have left the masculinism of this quote unaltered.
26 Hume, *Treatise on Human Nature*, xx.
27 In this regard the writer who has done most to demonstrate the way public feelings animate the Mass-Observation Archive is the pioneering historian, Claire Langhamer.

The following examples show the rich seam of feelings and emotions she has mined: '"The Live Dynamic Whole of Feeling and Behavior": Capital Punishment and the Politics of Emotion, 1945–1957', *Journal of British Studies* 51, no. 2 (2012): 416–41; *The English in Love: The Intimate Story of an Emotional Revolution* (Oxford: Oxford University Press, 2013); 'Feelings, Women and Work in the Long 1950s', *Women's History Review* 26, no. 1 (2017): 77–92; 'Mass Observing the Atom Bomb: The Emotional Politics of August 1945', *Contemporary British History* 33, no. 2 (2019): 208–25.

28 Tom Harrisson, 'What Is Public Opinion?', *Political Quarterly* 11 (1940): 368.
29 Mass-Observation, *Mass-Observation*, this volume, 46.
30 Mass-Observation, *Mass-Observation*, this volume, 45.
31 Mass-Observation, *Mass-Observation*, this volume, 46.
32 Mass-Observation, *Mass-Observation*, this volume, 50.
33 Mass-Observation, *Mass-Observation*, this volume, 49–50. Sets of image cards were never produced, or if prototypes were trialled no such sets remain.
34 Mass-Observation, 'Poetic Description and Mass-Observation', *New Verse*, no. 24 (February–March 1937): 2 (italics in the original) and Mass-Observation, *Mass-Observation*, this volume, 52.
35 Mass-Observation, 'Poetic Description and Mass-Observation', 3.
36 Mass-Observation, 'Poetic Description and Mass-Observation', 2.
37 Mass-Observation, *Mass-Observation*, this volume, 51–2.
38 Humphrey Jennings and Charles Madge, eds., *May the Twelfth: Mass-Observation Day-Surveys 1937 (by over two hundred observers)* (London: Faber and Faber, 1987) (first published in 1937).
39 As one of their directives the national panel of voluntary observers were tasked with keeping a day diary on the 12th of each month. Given that one of the events that had sparked the emergence of MO was the constitutional crisis that led to the abdication of King Edward VIII, it is likely that the 12th was picked earlier in the year with the foreknowledge that it would also fall on the day of the Coronation.
40 Jennings and Madge, eds., *May the Twelfth*, iii.
41 Jennings and Madge, eds., *May the Twelfth*, iv.
42 Mass-Observation, *Mass-Observation*, this volume, 45.
43 Mass-Observation, *First Year's Work 1937–38*, 70.
44 Mass-Observation, *Mass-Observation*, this volume, 45.
45 Madge, 'Magic and Materialism', 33.
46 Madge, 'Magic and Materialism'. While Madge uses the male pronoun in a way that is no longer acceptable for a generic person it is worth noting that MO have always recruited more women than men.
47 The press coverage of the pamphlet was extensive and was reviewed in daily papers such as the *Daily Express* and *Evening Standard* as well as in magazines like *Left*

Review. The press coverage of the pamphlet and the first MO book (*May the Twelfth*) is extensively collected and analysed in *First Year's Work 1937–38*, 48–63.

48   Jennings and Madge, eds. *May the Twelfth*, iii.

49   Mass-Observation, *First Year's Work 1937–38*, 63.

50   See Mark Toogood, 'Modern Observations: New Ornithology and the Science of Ourselves, 1920–1940', *Journal of Historical Geography* 37, no. 3 (2011): 348–57 and Charles Withers and Diarmid Finnegan, 'Natural History Societies, Fieldwork and Local Knowledge in Nineteenth-century Scotland: Towards a Historical Geography of Civic Science', *Cultural Geographies* 10, no. 3 (2003): 334–53.

51   Charles Madge, 'Anthropology at Home', *The New Statesman and Nation* (January 2, 1937): 12.

52   http://www.bbc.co.uk/videonation/history/birth.shtml – accessed 3 February 2021.

53   Nico Carpentier, 'The BBC's Video Nation as a Participatory Media Practice: Signifying Everyday Life, Cultural Diversity and Participation in an Online Community', *International Journal of Cultural Studies* 6, no. 4 (2003): 425–47.

2

Mass-Observation

MASS-OBSERVATION SERIES

Number One
MASS-OBSERVATION
By
CHARLES MADGE &
TOM HARRISSON
With a Foreword by
PROFESSOR JULIAN HUXLEY
London
FREDERICK MULLER, LTD.
29 Great James St W.C.1

FOREWORD

By Professor Julian Huxley[1]

Science in its progress is advancing nearer to the human heart of things. The first great advances in the scientific renaissance were made in the remoter and simpler fields of astronomy and physics. Then followed chemistry and a little later general biology and physiology. The great revolution in regard to individual psychology did not take place until well into the present century. Now it is the turn of the most complex of all the sciences, sociology, which is also the nearest home, since we live immersed in society as a fish in water, and our ways of thinking and feeling are moulded by the social framework.

Within the social sciences, social anthropology holds an essential place. Yet, with few exceptions, it has started to choose its material from among primitive and out-of-the-way peoples. Here again the trend must be from the remote to the near at hand. Not only scientifically but practically it is urgent to obtain detailed and unbiased information as to the mode of thinking of the larger, more powerful and economically more important groups of human beings. Most urgent of all is to obtain such knowledge about our own group, the English people.

Science has a twofold task – to know and to control. Some sort of scientific control of society, in place of the unscientific game of politics and the mere play of impersonal economic forces, is overdue: and we shall not obtain any efficient measure of control unless this is grounded in adequate knowledge. For this reason the technique of Mass-Observation, here set forth by its inventors, seems to me of great value; for it does aim at disclosing ourselves to ourselves by the application of scientific methods of observation and record.

At the beginning of such a study the work must, necessarily, be almost entirely empirical. In this respect it may be compared with a good deal of bird-watching and natural history observation; and, largely because of its empiricism it has, like them, room for the untrained 'amateur' just as readily as the trained scientist. In fact, some of the 'day-surveys' I have seen, made by observers with no scientific training, would put many orthodox scientists to shame in their simplicity, clearness and objectivity.

Another valuable feature of Mass-Observation is that it stimulates and vivifies the observers. Many observers have noted that they are stimulated to take an interest in things and ideas which they had previously taken for granted. It creates a band of socially minded and scientifically minded people within the community at large. In many cases an actual day's work on Mass-Observation seems to exhaust people to an unexpected extent, and yet, I am told, they come up for more.

I will not comment on the details of the scheme, except to say that I was extremely interested in the project for discovering more about the possibilities for a broad social outlet for art. Nothing could well be more valuable than to contribute towards ending the present divorce between the artist and society at large, and towards initiating a period of truly socialized art.

I commend this pamphlet to the attention of the intelligent public, and hope that out of it big things will grow.

The Zoological Society of London, N.W.8
May 1937

Notes

1   Foreword to Mass Observation by Julian Huxley reprinted by permission of Peters Fraser & Dunlop (www.petersfraserdunlop.com) on behalf of the Estate of Julian Huxley.

NOTE

This pamphlet was produced with the help of many people besides the authors. Among them were Guy Hunter, who wrote reports on organizations similar to our own, and Humphrey Jennings, who also designed the cover. The draft was read through by several eminent scientists and writers, and their criticism was of the highest value. So was the criticism of technicians and workers, both men and women, with whom the ideas were threshed out.

Mass-Observation is organized from 6 Grote's Buildings, Blackheath, London, S.E.3, and all inquiries should be sent to that address. If after reading the pamphlet you should wish to co-operate by becoming a Mass-Observer, send a card and instructions will be forwarded to you.

January–April 1937
T. H.
C. M.

THE KING WANTS TO MARRY MRS SIMPSON: CABINET ADVISES 'NO'

I

Confronted with these headlines, a nation of fifty millions gasped in astonishment. Institutions which had been accepted as part of the course of nature were now thrown open to question. The fixation to the symbolism of monarchy which had been so abundantly displayed at the Jubilee of King George V, and again at his death, was now shocked into awareness of itself. At last England had to face a situation to which there was no stock response. Millions of people who passed their lives as the obedient automata of a system now had to make a personal choice, almost for the first time since birth.

Perhaps some of them had read Frazer's description of a primitive king. 'He lives hedged in by ceremonious etiquette, a network of prohibitions and observances, of which the intention is not to contribute to his dignity, much less to his comfort, but to restrain him from conduct which, by disturbing the harmony of nature, might involve himself, his people and the universe in one common catastrophe.'[1] Perhaps as they observed the reactions of their friends and neighbours in face of the 'crisis', they marvelled at the open emergence of forces so powerful, and realized as never before the sway of superstition in the midst of science. How little we know of our next door neighbour and his habits; how little we know of ourselves. Of conditions of life and thought in another class or another district, our ignorance is complete. The anthropology of ourselves is still only a dream. It is left to the intuitions of men of genius to cope with the unknown mass. Such intuitions are to a human science of the future what cookery is to chemistry. The building up of such a science is an urgent problem for mankind.

It was with thoughts like these that a group of people started *Mass-Observation*, which aims to be a scientific study of human social behaviour, beginning at home. Such a study has already been begun by anthropologists in the case of primitive peoples, and tentatively by psychologists and sociologists in civilized countries. But in the latter case, the field to be covered is so vast and so apparently nebulous that the scientists have little more to offer than generalizations on method.

Mass-Observation intends to work with a new method. It intends to make use not only of the trained scientific observer, but of the untrained observer, the man in the street. Ideally, it is the observation by everyone of everyone, including themselves. The present pamphlet is designed to explain this method to a wider public than those Observers who are already engaged on it, and to invite the co-operation of all who agree that a science of ourselves is a crying necessity of to-day.

The bringing of 'civilization' to Abyssinia, the coming of civil war to Spain, the atavism of the new Germany and the revival of racial superstition have forced the issue home to many. We are all in danger of extinction from such outbursts of atavism. We look to science to help us, only to find that science is too busy forging new weapons of destruction to give heed to our questions. But despair need not drive us back into ways of thought which science has replaced. For some this has seemed the only solution – a return to the past offered as an alternative to the scientific use of the present. This pamphlet takes the opposite view. It assumes that the contemporary attitude of doubt is not the end of the epoch of science, but the beginning of a new epoch of science.

Analogies have been pointed out between the curious customs of the savage, and the customs, familiar but no less curious, which prevail at home. Psychiatrists have noted the resemblance between those in asylums and those outside. Such analogies have a disturbing effect, because they point to certain things which are common to all men in virtue of being men. Science, however, can take no account of this embarrassment and the subsequent hostility to further inquiry. Having pressed the analogies so far, science must go on to apply the same inquiry in every human sphere, above all in the sphere nearest home. It is the task of science not to pass a moral judgement on superstition, but simply to examine and describe it, leaving to others to decide whether they want if or not.*

* *Definition of 'superstition'* (in H. C. Warren's Dictionary of Psychology, London, 1935).

1. a disposition or tendency to ascribe phenomena which admit of a natural explanation to occult or supernatural causes;
2. a belief or practice which manifests this tendency;
3. an accepted belief whose falsity has been scientifically demonstrated.

Strictly, it is incorrect to apply the term to primitive attempts at scientific knowledge, or the adjective to individuals who lived before the falsity of these primitive beliefs was demonstrated.

II

If it is a million years since man was differentiated from the apes, and 450,000 years since the appearance of Homo Sapiens, it is 6,000 years since the beginning of the Osiris civilization in Egypt, 500 years since the rise of the bourgeoisie and 150 years since the industrial revolution. The rate of change has been accelerated. Science has produced its astonishing effects on the earth's surface at an accelerating speed.

From the first, man differed from the animals in being more scientific than they. But in addition to science, he began in one of his earliest phases to produce magical and religious systems whose effect in general has been to impede the development of science. Periods which have been sceptical about established systems, in particular of established magical and religious systems, have been correspondingly fruitful for science. In our own times, science appears to have triumphed, but has not by any means altogether superseded the pre-scientific systems of thought and behaviour.

In surveying the field of superstition in 1937, much is visible whose roots go back not only hundreds but thousands of years, back even to the earliest days of prehistoric man. Such superstitions everyone is agreed to call by that name, but there are others which have assumed modern disguises and escape recognition. It is comparatively easy in some cases to recognize the ancestry of modern superstitions; it is easy, for example, to see the connection between spiritualism and the primitive belief in ghosts, or between the modern mascot and the primitive totem. But spiritualists would deny that they were superstitious, and indeed cannot be assumed to be so until it can be proved that they are not scientific. The users of mascots likewise would deny that they were superstitious, or would say that they were superstitious only in jest. However, their reaction to having the mascot taken away from them might betray that they believed in it more than they knew. To give examples of active superstition is difficult, because if the superstition is active, a percentage of people believe in it, and this percentage will refuse to admit that they are superstitious until they are scientifically proved to be so. The modern equivalents of the corroboree, of human sacrifice, of sympathetic magic have got to be detected in the midst of innovations which seem completely at variance with ideas of magic, of savagery, of the supernatural.

Superstition is infinitely adaptable. Although the process of adaptation has been continuous, it has never been more striking than during the last hundred years – a century notable for vast social and mechanical changes, and an unprecedented increase in population. New tools, like the pointed screw, and new weapons, like the firearm, have repercussions on the whole of society. Such revolutionary inventions have been especially numerous during the past hundred years. The steam railway, the spinning jenny, electric power, photography, have had so great an impact on mental and physical behaviour that we are barely conscious of it. Those who have attempted to convey an impression of what this impact has been like have been reduced to abandoning all coherence and realism, and have fled in the direction of the interior life or of the abstract form. Some reminiscences and diaries, some realistic novels, have provided a fragmentary picture, but always from a personal angle or from the angle of romance. A description in scientific terms of the changes in modes of living during the nineteenth century is unachieved. A similar description for our own day is practically unattempted.

Take the example of the railway. Not only did it create a new architecture, and a new type of engineer, a new culture of the railway ticket and the railway station – but it altered irrevocably the nature of dreams and of childish fantasy (ambition to be an engine driver). If any reader thinks: 'But we know all that', he should think again. We all know how to use the railway in our daily life; but what we do not realize is the power of the railway to modify our lives when we are not using it. It has given us a different conception of space, of speed and of power. It has rendered possible mass activities – the Cup Final, the monster rally, the seaside holiday, the hiking excursion – whose ramifying effects on our behaviour and mentality extend almost beyond imagination.

The more recent acquisitions – electricity, the aeroplane, the radio – are so new that the process of adaptation to them is still going on. It is within the scope of the science of *Mass-Observation* to watch the process taking place – perhaps to play some part in determining the adaptation of old superstitions to new conditions. These forces are so new and so terrific that they are commonly thought of as kinds of magic power that can only be wielded by a few men, the technicians. Hence there is a widespread fatalism among the mass about present and possible future effects of science, and a tendency to leave them alone as beyond the scope of the intervention of the common man. The technician, on the other hand, is not concerned with the implications of his activity or its effect on the masses.

This fatalism reaches its extreme in the general attitude to war and scientific methods of destruction. The fear of air-raids and gas is part of the general fear of what science may do next – exemplified in popular myths about a death-ray. The fear of gas especially – the all-pervasive death which attacks all classes and all sections, combatants and non-combatants, and against which all defence is probably useless – brings with it that doubt and scepticism and despair from which our inquiry starts. But doubts of science, because it can thus deal death, may take either a scientific or an antiscientific shape. Gas and the bomber, most modern of scientific products, are therefore calculated to make acute the controversy between science and superstition. The controversy becomes a very simple one: which gives us most hope of surviving?

There must be an enormous number of people in this country who are aware of this dilemma in some degree – aware of it rather than fully conscious. Only a small minority are capable of expressing the dilemma in its logical terms. But since everyone can read and write, it is impossible under modern conditions to withhold the real issues from the majority indefinitely. 'Their's not to reason why' was a feasible attitude to adopt towards an illiterate slave population, but is feasible no longer. The literate mass of to-day is a phenomenon unique in the history of human cultures. But countering the effects of literacy on the mass, there is a continuous supply of automatic thinking and foregone conclusions appearing as spontaneous thinking and voluntary conclusions.

It was the industrial revolution which led to the literate mass. There was previously no need for the serf or agricultural labourer to read, and at first it was thought that the less-skilled section of the working-class could profitably be left uneducated. This proved to be an illusion, and literacy for all became a generally recognized necessity, which the Education Act of 1870 was intended to bring about. Widely diffused journals and penny libraries continued the work of primary education. An acquaintance with the general principles of science spread rapidly through what had been previously the most ignorant section of the population.

It is generally agreed that the industrial revolution had a disruptive effect on the morals and belief of the working class. The temperance movements and the Friendly Societies provided an alternative to desperation and excess. Two types of working man grew up side by side, often in the same family and beneath the same roof: the hard-drinking, hard-swearing, wage-spending type, untroubled by qualms of religion or morality, and the teetotal, religious, wage-saving type, who aimed by self-discipline at providing his children with the chance of escaping from the environment. It is only gradually that the prolongation of industrialism has made more numerous a third type who has looked for a solution in terms of science rather than of religion. A similar attempt to rationalize the social attitude towards sex and to put men and women on a footing of social equality has also gained ground since the turn of the century.

Another factor of basic importance in all investigation is the availability of the entire mass, through its literacy, to suggestion for commercial, political or other reasons. The history of mass-advertising dates back before the 'seventies. Since 1900 the daily newspaper, the radio and the film have all been busily cultivating the enormous field, until now a peak of mass-publicizing has been reached. Primary and secondary education have rendered the vastly increased population accessible to the persuasion of words written and spoken, and accompanying pictorial images and musical sounds. Staffs of technical experts are kept continuously employed in devising new methods of persuasion, and it is an axiom of publicity that entertainment – stage, film, fiction, radio, etc. – carries the propaganda message far more effectively than open advertisement. Entertainment gets past the defences of those who resist more obvious forms of suggestion, and is therefore the vehicle of suggestion most highly esteemed by the specialists.

People now aged between fifty and sixty were brought up to regard as a familiar object the tobacco carton on which the bearded sailor is inset in a lifebelt against a sunset sea.[2] Such an image has acquired over half a century some of the force which has made the flag, the heraldic emblem and the religious icon, symbols of permanence and social inevitability. The children who attended the first primary schools saw on the walls advertisements for mustard, matches and chocolate – together with samples of these products in process of manufacture, provided free by the manufacturer – while the music sheets which they used because they were distributed gratis each bore the name of a brand of pills. In 1937, the advertising agencies and daily newspapers employ the best empirical anthropologists and psychologists of the country. These great organizations base their work on the assumption that the human mind is suggestible and they aim their suggestions at that part of the human mind in which the superstitious elements predominate.

It is commonly thought that art, science and philosophy possess some detachment from human weakness which enables them to rise above these superstitious elements and destroy them or at least counteract them. What, one may ask, has been the response of art, science and philosophy to this renewed challenge? Of the three philosophy has the least answer to give. It has tended to become more and more an aristocracy of thought whose beauty and detachment are those of anachronism rather than timelessness. Like fox-hunting, it is beautiful but out of date. Moreover, it has surrendered to science the right to dictate codes of manners and jurisprudence. Modern idealism and modern realism (in the technical philosophic senses) have been at pains to explain that they deal only with pure thought, and have no connection with life whatever. The pragmatist, or modern nominalist, is not concerned as were some of his predecessors with system building but only with system destroying and the demonstration that all the systems are the same. The various forms of materialism since 1830 have all tended to be the negation of philosophy rather than a development of it. Pure sensation, pure intuition, have been the bases of the most remarkable philosophies of modern times, those of Bergson and Croce. Their whole bias has been away from philosophy as knowledge and towards philosophy as aesthetics, or as a rarefied branch of art. None of the generalizations in this paragraph will satisfy the philosophers, secure in the midst of their systems: all that concerns us is that none of the systems they invoke has had sufficient force to stem the oceanic flux and reflux of the twentieth century.

The scientific study of superstition begins with the study of man, and of all the branches of science those which deal with man have developed last. All sciences have helped to make ready the moment at which the science of man could emerge. Copernicus and Galileo put an end to the view of things in which the whole universe depended on man. Anatomists and physiologists aided by the researches of chemists and the classification of zoologists began to dissect and analyse the human body in increasing detail. The other physical sciences, by contributing to the industrial revolution, hastened on the impending discoveries. It was the industrial revolution which made scientific expeditions all over the world a practical necessity, and which sent Charles Darwin with H.M.S. *Beagle* on a voyage round the world.

Darwin was sent out as a geologist. It was geology, as exemplified in Lyell, which brought to notice the antiquity of the earth, the fossils of extinct animals and the unhistoric character of the commonly accepted Bible story of the Creation. In South America Darwin saw gigantic fossils embedded in the side of cliffs. In the Galapagos Islands he saw the fauna of those islands to be unique, and yet more closely related to the fauna of South America, the nearest mainland, than to any other. In Tierra del Fuego, his first glimpse of man under really primitive conditions made a deep impression on him. From these concrete experiences, joined to a lifetime of research, he elaborated his epoch-changing theories. First, the theory of the origin of the different animal and vegetable species by a gradual evolution over millions of years. Secondly, in corollary to this, the descent of man himself from animal ancestors. Thirdly, as an inevitable consequence, the survival in man, to a degree he has never been willing to admit, of his original animal nature. These theories he set out in three great works, the *Origin of Species*, *Descent of Man* and *Expression of Emotions in Man and Animals*.

Never before had science presented so revolutionary a picture of man in relation to the universe. Yet amid the strongest opposition, the picture continued to gain wider and wider acceptance. Men like Huxley devoted their lives to fostering the scientific attitude towards man. In the sociological sphere Marx pays tribute to Darwin as his great forerunner. His work also made possible the new science of anthropology, which E. B. Tylor was inaugurating in the 'sixties. Another pioneer in the investigation of the human animal, Sigmund Freud, records in his autobiography that he was led to scientific studies by reading Darwin.

Darwin made it possible to ask questions about man which had hitherto only been asked about other animals. He is therefore the parent of all subsequent investigations about man. The investigations have proceeded on divergent lines. Controversies have arisen, and have raged fiercely, all the more so when the status of man was at stake. Such theories as those of Marx and Freud have been felt to raise questions so fundamental that they were moral issues and therefore outside the pale of science. Though neither Freud nor Marx can be neglected in a study of the science of man, they have neither of them reached the acceptance among scientists that Charles Darwin has done. Yet both have become part of the intellectual stock-in-trade of the period, and are significant of an ultimate convergence of science with art and politics.

Since Tylor (himself by no means free from personal superstitions) began to collect facts about the customs and behaviour of primitive man, a vast amount of fieldwork has been done all over the world, and various theories erected on the data obtained. As is usual in the early stages of a science, none of these theories has held ground for long undisputed. The facts are still of greater importance than the theories. These facts have in practice an intrinsic interest for us which is due to their coming from a less materially complicated human environment than ours. They lead us to believe that we see in them the simplified image of ourselves.

In the foreground of the picture which anthropology presents is the widespread practice of magic. From the first Tylor seems to have been aware of the part which magical ideas still play in civilized communities, as when he writes: 'By a vast mass of evidence from savage, barbaric and civilised life, magic arts which have resulted from mistaking an ideal for a real connection may be clearly traced from the lower culture which they are of to the higher culture which they are in.' No more complete study of magic has been compiled than Frazer's monumental *Golden Bough*. Frazer looks on magic as a kind of primitive or 'bastard' science. Subsequent anthropology has shown this to be a doubtful generalization. According to the *Encyclopædia Britannica* (14th Edition): 'Primitive man has his real science running side by side with his magic. The two are closely bound together in the practical application, the body of rational knowledge being utilised to deal with the mechanical efficiency of the undertaking, while the ritual of magic deals with the incalculable elements therein the luck and chance on which so much of success depends.' In other words, man only uses magic as a second line of attack. Having taken all the reasonable precautions to ensure success, he goes on to take unreasonable precautions. But when he finds out new scientific precautions which are better than the magical ones, he may be prepared to abandon the latter. A magical prescription in this view precedes a scientific prescription for the same purpose, and in this sense Frazer's account still holds good.

But it must be accepted that science is as old as magic. There is a great deal in modern life which corresponds with this function of magic as second line of attack. Art can be considered in this light. An age of great scientific discoveries is favourable to art, because it is continually raising new questions, and art attempts to answer these questions in its own way, before science is ready to answer them in the scientific way. This was particularly true of art in the nineteenth century, the great century of scientific discoveries about man. Industrial development, and the resulting social changes, laid a great nervous strain on the individual. It is on the individual and his introspections that the stress of nineteenth-century art is placed. Curiously enough, these introspections, when they are not about personal emotional conflicts, struck a rich mine of anthropological material. It was a period of sudden illuminations which seemed to lay bare the inmost secrets of human nature. Such a succession of insights as is contained in Rimbaud's *Illuminations*:

J'ai seul la cle de cette parade sauvage[3] is a pre-scientific parallel to the successive discoveries about the unconscious mind made in the course of Freudian psycho-analysis. Artists soon perceived the analogy between what they were discovering about themselves and the simultaneous discoveries about primitive man and neurotic man. Many modern poets and painters have turned instinctively to anthropology and psycho-analysis as their sources. The result has not been altogether happy. By the same natural law which makes magic obsolete when science produces an alternative method, art cannot successfully compete with science on the same ground. All that such art can hope to effect is to make clear to other artists the immense importance of science. Because Rimbaud precedes Freud, his works have a historical significance far beyond those of the post-Freudian surrealist writers and painters. Only Marcel Duchamp has taken the logical step of continuing his work as a scientist, instead of using science as material for art, and Duchamp's gesture has been lost on a world which can see no difference between his experiments on optics and those of the professional physicist.

Whenever it becomes historically necessary for man to view the world in a new way, artists will arise who are sensitive to the change and will display to man the world which science will then proceed to classify and interpret. Perhaps the two functions – displaying the world and classifying it – are for the time being no longer divisible. In certain branches of science and of art, the individual scientist or artist becomes absorbed in a collective activity which is purely human in type and which excludes neither of the two categories. There is no laboratory big enough to hold the whole of science.

It is not the purpose of this pamphlet to go more fully into the rich and complicated history of thought during the past hundred years. In particular the suggestions about art are made without any attempt at detail. Only a handful claim to understand the modern development of art. If, as this pamphlet is content to hint, art descends again from the clouds which now hide it, and is once more generally intelligible, it will in the meantime have undergone a transformation into something more akin to science than hitherto. The details of that transformation will become clear in the course of time. But the important point to emphasize at this stage is the possibility for the artist and the scientist to meet on common ground. The work of the greatest artists has always been akin to that of the greatest scientists. Both look at the world in the same realistic way. In the nineteenth century Tolstoy and Courbet developed a realism essentially like that of science, though they never made any conscious approximation of their art to the method of science. They were observers and describers of a subject-matter which at that time ran alongside the subject-matter of science but had not yet merged with it. At the time that this pamphlet is being written, art and science are both turning towards the same field: the field of human behaviour which lies immediately before our eyes.

To sum up, the arrival on the scene of Mass-Observation seems to coincide:

1. with a poverty of philosophy
2. with the close of an epoch of illuminations of the inner man by art
3. with the centenary of the development of scientific methods for studying man, which still wait mass-application.

We saw also that the discovery of new material forces had reached a suicidal point in the form of poison gas; and that a new technique for making use of the superstitiousness of a literate but suggestible majority was being brought to final perfection. This, then, is the point at which Mass-Observation was founded and the present pamphlet written.

(January 1937)

III

How does Mass-Observation propose to go to work?

The field is vast, the task of collecting data is long and difficult. On these data science will one day build new hypotheses and theories. In the meantime, we must patiently amass material, without unduly prejudging or preselecting from the total number of available facts. All this material, all the reports from our observers, carefully filed, will be a reference library accessible to every genuine research worker.

But for this labour there are immediate compensations. It will encourage people to look more closely at their social environment than ever before and will place before them facts about other social environments of which they know little or nothing. This will effectively contribute to an increase in the general social consciousness. It will counteract the tendency so universal in modern life to perform all our actions through sheer habit, with as little consciousness of our surroundings as though we were walking in our sleep. Even the drab and sordid features of industrial life will take on a new interest when they become the subject of scientific observation. His squalid boarding house will become for the observer what the entrails of the dog-fish are to the zoologist the material of science and source of its *divina voluptas*. Not for nothing has the detective become a figure of popular admiration: his is a profession which calls for a scientific analysis of human motives and behaviour. In the detection which we intend to practise, there is no criminal and all human beings are of equal interest. We do not intend to intrude on the private life of any individual, as individual. Collective habits and social behaviour are our field of inquiry, and individuals are only of interest in so far as they are typical of groups.

Moreover, Mass-Observation shares the interest of most people in the actual, in what happens from day to day. Every day the social consciousness is modified by the news reported in the newspapers and on the wireless. The more exciting the news, the more unified does the social consciousness become in its absorption with a single theme. The abdication of King Edward VIII was a focusing point of this kind. The coronation of King George VI is providing another. At such times, our observers will each be watching the social reactions within their own local environment. They will be the meteorological stations from whose reports a weather-map of popular feeling can be compiled. A survey of this kind was made by twenty-five observers on 12 February 1937, a normal day on which nothing of importance took place; another survey is being made on 12th May, the date of the Coronation, and an abnormal day in social life and consciousness. These surveys will be published. They give an extraordinary picture of England – extraordinary, though the material they report is completely ordinary.

(a) The Observer

The Observer will not need to have received scientific training in order to make his observations. He will make them in the course of his ordinary work, using to the full the environment in which he normally works. His function will be to describe fully, clearly, and in simple language all that he sees and hears in connection with the specific problem he is asked to work on.

Everything will depend on the reliability of such an Observer compared with that of the trained scientist. In science the ideal observer is as objective as a machine. But when it comes to dealing with human behaviour, even the scientist finds it impossible to rule out his own subjective bias. With our untrained Observers we must expect this to be even more marked. Feelings will interfere in the choice of facts and method of approach, especially through the unconscious omission of certain facts. It is seldom that there is any chance of knowing what personal bias is likely to have affected the findings of scientists; but in the case of the Observers, we aim at having sufficient cross-references about them to indicate the probable nature of the bias in each individual. We want the Observers themselves to give us these cross-references, and if possible to have them corroborated by someone else. To write objective reports comes naturally to some, to others calls for a process of self-schooling. The first task of an Observer is to write an objective report on himself.

The scientist almost inevitably suffers from a bias towards the academic. In his laboratory he is isolated from his fellow men. For the study of many problems such detachment may be of benefit, but in the study of human behaviour it is a serious handicap. But when we leave his atmosphere of detachment and seek observers in the everyday world, we find there every other kind of bias imaginable. Class, race, locality each breeds its own bias which may take the form of religious, intellectual or political prejudice. But it is this which makes a system of conflicting observers useful, and no observer useless. It is desirable that opposed persons should observe and report the same phenomena. So it is essential that Mass-Observation should recruit from all classes, from all localities and from every shade of opinion. Only those who are afraid of knowing the facts or of letting them be known will refuse to co-operate or prove avowedly hostile. And against all such hostility, objective method is the best defence.

Already, differences within the initial group have been a fruitful source of new ideas and new methods of approach. Provided they do not lead to the formation of factions such differences will continue to be our life-blood and the guarantee that we do not become incapable of development. The suggestions of some hundred people are by now incorporated in the framework of Mass-Observation and by this process it must grow. Mutual give and take between those who formulate the inquiries and the Observers who have to carry them out should help to safeguard against a set of one-sided questions yielding merely a one-sided set of answers. Fixed ideas in the investigators have a way of automatically cooking the results even where there is every wish to be objective. For that reason we wish also for criticism of this pamphlet. Every criticism will play a part in what must by definition be a co-operative effort to build a science which shall truly be science for all.

(b) The scientific expert

The researches of the scientific expert will be in no way displaced by the enrolment of an army of observers. His work remains an essential corollary. Mass-Observation needs the active co-operation of the scientists; even when they are too busy with their own researches to co-operate actively, there must be some method of co-ordination between our work and theirs, to prevent any experiment of ours from interfering with researches in fields where they have prior claim.

We want the assistance of trained scientists in drawing up the ground-plan for our long-term researches. It is for them to help in framing well-constructed hypotheses to be tested by Mass-Observation methods, and to suggest subjects for detailed inquiry. Our starting point is what they have already achieved, and we offer them a new instrument, with every opportunity to use it to the full.

Our first concern is to collect data, not to interpret them. But it is open to any scientist to make use of these data, and to produce his interpretation. After he has made it, the data will continue to be available for other interpreters. It is desirable that different interpretations of the same material should be published together, so as to indicate different possible points of view. In the sciences of human behaviour there are many schools. We do not want to attach ourselves exclusively to any school, but we want to give Freudian and behaviourist, functionalist and diffusionist, equal opportunity of using our results.

Anonymity is essential to Mass-Observation, and much of the scientific assistance given to it must necessarily be anonymous. But experts eminent in anthropology and psychology are lending us their critical guidance and helping to train the Observers along scientific lines.

The work of the professional scientist helps to give us a more rigorous objectivity. So also can the use of scientific instruments of precision. Photography, film technique, sound recording and physiological tests by experts will provide a check on our observations. We shall collaborate in building up museums of sound, smell, foods, clothes, domestic objects, advertisements, newspapers, etc. We shall also build up files dealing with problems of assimilation – the practical difficulties of an observer in entering a new environment. He should be able to hear records of dialects which are strange to him.[4] He should even be able to find in a 'field wardrobe' the necessary outfit of clothing for effective assimilation.

The three sciences most immediately relevant to Mass-Observation are psychology, anthropology and sociology. It is their work which has made a project like ours thinkable. Yet each of these sciences has admittedly many limitations; to other scientists they are apt to seem outside the sphere of exact science. For example, the anthropologist makes his observations unchecked. He can see and say what he likes. In writing up his material he repeatedly mixes up fact and interpretation of fact. His observations are not repeated. When an anthropologist has been to a place, that place is considered 'done'. No account is taken of the anthropologist's personal bias, politics, religion, etc., though these are manifestly relevant. He lives among strange people and learns to speak their language; but it is not considered necessary for him to learn to dance their dances, eat their diet or love their women – factors at least as important as language in understanding other people. He neglects biology, ecology, statistical, physiological, climatic and geological factors.

Psychology is a wide term which includes many lines of approach to the study of human behaviour. Psychologists themselves are realizing increasingly the need for a study of normal social psychology. Good work has been done in Austria and in the United States, and in Britain several groups have been preparing the ground for the past few years. Psychology, like anthropology, is split up into warring sects – a symptom in itself that these sciences are as yet in an early stage of development. For us the work of psycho-analyst and psychiatrist is of equal interest with that of the behaviourist and the intelligence-tester.

In sociology the social surveys, such as those in London and Liverpool, provide much necessary statistical material. But no social survey in this country has tackled the ordinary behaviour, superstitions and ideas of those surveyed. In America, Middletown was an attempt of this sort. Perhaps the best work on these lines so far is a study of the unemployed at Marienthal in Austria.[5]

But though it is easy to pick holes in the work of these sciences, the important point to remember is that in all of them and in many other sciences and fields of thought, there is a growing tendency to approximate to the aims which Mass-Observation sets itself. The idea is already widely established: we only seek to provide the instrument.

(c) Other experts

In a previous section it was said that it was now possible for the artist and the scientist to meet on common ground. We wish to put this assertion to a practical test. The man in the street is apt to complain of art that it is not useful to him, does not supply him with anything he really wants. Art has become too highly specialized for mass-consumption. Yet every ornament on his mantelpiece is a proof that he needs some satisfaction beyond that which the pots and pans in his kitchen can provide. Mass-Observation is going to try to find out what this basic need is, and then if possible to get the artists to satisfy it.

The first necessity is to make people more conscious of their own wishes. Why do they choose one calendar rather than another? Why do they read one novel, or see one film, rather than another? Often enough they cannot answer such simple questions, yet there must be an answer.

Pictures play a continual part in our lives, though often unrealized. We intend to issue series of images, like packs of playing cards, and to suggest various exercises which can be played with them. These exercises will be designed to sharpen the powers of observation of a particular type – the observation of images. Just as Pelmanism is designed to strengthen the memory, so these exercises will strengthen the imagination.[6] The use in this connection of the word 'image' may seem to the psychologist an arbitrary one, and requires definition. The image, in our sense, is something between an idea and a sensation. It is more vivid than an abstract idea; it is more intangible than a concrete sensation. A card in this pack will be a piece of paper which has the property of suggesting an image – of a skeleton, of a house with broken windows. Pictures have this power of suggesting images; so have words. For example:

A HOUSE WITH BROKEN WINDOWS

Painting is concerned with images in the form of pictures; poetry with images in the form of words. The poet and painter are experts in the conscious use of images. Some people possess this faculty in a high degree; others hardly at all. The same image has an infinite number of uses, because it can 'stand for' an infinite number of things. A preliminary exercise on the images in the pack would be to ask yourself the following questions:

1. Describe each in a few words.
2. Which makes most impression on you?
3. In which of them do you find elements that suggest: home, food, nature, life, death, science, sex?
4. What important element do you feel to be missing?
5. What other images would you add, to make the set complete (a) for you personally (b) for people generally?
6. Which do you like best? Which do you dislike most?
7. What common elements can you find in all of them?
8. Which image or images seem most typical of the day on which you are making the test?
9. What period of history does each image suggest?

(d) Presenting the results

The scientist engaged in research prefers to work in isolation and without publicity until he has completed his investigation. He has many good reasons for his attitude. When his results are ready, he is glad to lecture on them, and to publish them in scientific journals; but the lectures are usually only for university students, and the journals are only read by specialists like himself. If his results do ever win a wider publicity, they will be diffused in the form of 'popular science' and will have become in the process so diluted as to be of little value. As it is diffused for mass-consumption, the work of the scientist reassumes the very superstitiousness which it was to supersede. Individual scientists deplore this state of affairs, but there is nothing they can do about it, so long as the mass remains so naturally superstitious that it will only swallow science in the form of superstition.

Mass-Observation has got to tackle this problem at its roots. To make the scheme work, not only must facts be collected over the widest possible field, but they must be made known to the widest possible public. This double objective makes of *Mass-Observation* not only a science but something more than science has hitherto been. Questions of mass-organization and mass-publicity have to be confronted: thence arise questions of style and presentation. The facts must be made accessible in plain English which everyone can understand. This is a science which can only work if it is kept free from scientific jargon, and also from the obscurity typical of the contemporary artist and intellectual. It has also to avoid the facile temptations of popular exposition. The entire population is impregnated with a catch-word culture ceaselessly diffused by the written and spoken word. Only the completely objective fact can escape the ill-effects of such treatment. The idea, being more abstract, is a hundred times delayed or illegitimized before it reaches at fifth hand the ultimate consumer, the ordinary man who has no defence against what he is told. The lesson is to stick to facts, and to set them down as intelligibly as is humanly possible.

This pamphlet is necessary as a preliminary statement. It is a first step towards a future statement intended for a more universal audience and based not on speculations but on practical results. The first publications of *Mass-Observation* are bound to be incompletely representative of the masses to whom its studies are addressed. Until the observers are sufficiently numerous and representative of every class and section, this incompleteness will remain.

This is the first of a series of projected publications. Other pamphlets will deal with such questions as 'What are your superstitions?', 'Why do you watch birds?', 'What is on your mantelpiece?', 'What do you mean by freedom?' These will be collective books, based on the work of the Observers. They will be issued as cheaply as possible, to make them generally available. As soon as practicable, they will be followed by cheap editions of scientific works with an important bearing on *Mass-Observation*.

An indispensable aid to development will be a monthly bulletin, designed for wide circulation. It will be an experiment in co-operative newspaper-making, since those who read it will also help to write it. It will put to the test the 'readability' of material produced by amateur writers. Judging from material already sent in, the untrained observer has a real gift for reproducing incidents and conversations of human interest as well as scientific relevance, as illustrated in the following story from the report of a woman Observer:

'Coming home on a Midland Red bus from Birmingham (a distance of approx. 6 miles) I was sitting on the front seat, near the large sliding door. There was a cold easterly wind blowing through the door, and after having some cigarette ash blown in my eyes, I touched the conductor on the sleeve to attract his attention and said: "May we have the door closed, conductor?" He turned round and leant towards me in a confidential way, and then said in a most insolent manner: "Yes, when I'm ready to shut it!" I was too surprised to make any reply. The door remained open until I left the bus.'

This Observer had been asked to report on examples of the behaviour of superiors to subordinates and vice versa which came to her notice. She sent in a series of 36 stories of which that given above is a fair sample. As a piece of scientific observation, it is of value in drawing attention to a peculiar social relation – that between a public employee (the bus conductor) and an individual using a public service (the passenger). Which is the superior? Each is apt to assume superiority, and a conflict between wills may result. The readability of the material is also borne out in the reports sent in on 12th February.

Their fascination is akin to that of the realistic novel, with the added interest of being fact and not fiction. The most ordinary environment is rich in surprises, and in transcribing their environments the Observers reveal the ultimately surprising character of life itself. Whereas fiction provides an escape into worlds of wish fulfilment, where the mill-girl always ends by marrying the mill-owner, these reports start from an acceptance of the real conditions of existence, an acceptance of the reality principle, the principle of adult life and of a modern scientific society.

(e) Co-ordination

A central body co-ordinates the activities of *Mass-Observation*, sending the Observers details of the specific observations to be made and handling the reports they send in. The composition of this body will remain fluid until we can employ the best people for the job. Some members of it will be whole-time workers, others will act as advisers. The central office and filing system is at 6 Grote's Buildings, Blackheath, London, S.E.3. Centralization in London has its disadvantages. In the hybrid and unstable complex which is modern London, it is possible that the co-ordinating body will be out of touch with mass-conditions of life.

To insure against a predominance at the centre of intellectuals living in academic isolation, the co-ordinators must spend much time in mass-environments, visiting industrial areas and working there. There must be strong provincial centres, preferably not in the largest towns, many of which have the disadvantages of London without its advantages. We shall have to make a cultural survey of the British Isles. From the survey maps will be prepared, dividing the country into cultural zones in which to place our centres.

In some cases the local groups will make concentrated surveys of their areas, like the American survey of 'Middletown'. In the Middletown survey, a small number of trained scientists visited the town for a period to make their observations. In the local surveys undertaken by *Mass-Observation*, the observers will not be visiting anthropologists, but the 'natives' themselves. The anthropology of whites requires an unusual objectivity, which can only be assured by covering the whole of the ground. Here science has to deal not with a tribal system with comparatively few deviations, but with a vast nebulous organization of individually varying habits, superstitions, obsessions, only held together by the economic framework of modern society. Therefore not only must the greatest possible number of people be studied, but the greatest possible number of people must help in the observations. England is divided into local cultures of great distinctness. It is also stratified into a large number of subtly graded class cultures. Furthermore, gulfs separate from each other the various professions. There is little contact between specialists in science and technology, and the fields of art and science are felt to be mutually exclusive. Each sectional bias has to be overcome before the technique of *Mass-Observation* can be effectively applied. A group of Observers in an industrial town in Lancashire has already made considerable headway on a local survey. A book describing this culture is in course of preparation.

Mass-Observation begins at home, but it has international perspectives. Not only is it likely that parallel organizations will arise in the other civilized countries, but we are already enlisting Observers of all colours and races. The interchange of Observers between different countries and different races is of even more far-reaching importance than interchange between Wigan and Bournemouth, between cotton mill and London office. To see ourselves as others see us is the first step towards objectivity about other races. In our survey of the Coronation, Chinese and Negro Observers will be watching the strange version of King-making which persists in the midst of western innovations. They come from countries where Kingship was no anachronism till western influence subverted and destroyed it.

The problems of co-ordination will grow greater with time. The immediate problem is to mobilize a numerous and representative corps of Observers, and to equip and maintain an efficient central organization, in touch with all other relevant research bodies, however different their methods. A list of such bodies is given below.[7] Financial support is necessary, but can only be accepted on the same terms as any other scientific grant, namely without expectation of any personal benefit by the donor. We shall not make specific requests for money from our Observers. Once under weigh, *Mass-Observation* should be self-supporting. Publicity is integral in the launching of any mass-movement but there is no need here to strain for effect. Slow development, gradual mobilization and avoidance of emotional or revivalist appeal are essential to the building up of a scientific organization.

(f) Basis for a Mass-Movement

We have little doubt that Mass-Observation will win the necessary support. It is an organization which has arisen in response to a common need, and provided it is efficient it will succeed. A scientific knowledge of their own social environment, habits, behaviour, and those of forty to fifty million others, is going to benefit most people. Their motives for wanting the knowledge will vary, and they will put it to different uses – in some cases to opposite and conflicting uses. Such knowledge could be of use both to the pacifist who wishes to prevent recruiting and to the War Office which wants to stimulate it. The advertising agency needs such knowledge to sell the products of its clients, and the man in the street needs the same knowledge to help prevent himself from being taken in by commercial or political propaganda. No scientist considers the consequences of his research at the time he is conducting his experiment; yet his work has social consequences and implications of far-reaching importance. Such implications will be bound to arise from the researches of *Mass-Observation*. What they will turn out to be is a matter of individual forecast and opinion. No two persons are likely to agree completely about them. The authors of this pamphlet have each his variant of opinion on the matter.

Tom Harrisson believes that *Mass-Observation*, by laying open to doubt all existing philosophies of life as possibly incomplete, yet by refusing to neglect the significance of any of them, may make a new synthesis. This may lead to something less fierce, more understanding and permanent, than the present miserable conflicts of dogmatic faiths in race, politics, religion. The whole study should cause us to reassess our inflated opinions of our progress and culture, altering our judgments on others accordingly. We must find the range of mass agreement and variation, the L.C.M. and H.C.F. of man, between which lie his practical potentialities.

In the other author's opinion, *Mass-Observation* is an instrument for collecting facts, not a means for producing a synthetic philosophy, a super-science or super-politics. The availability of the facts will liberate certain tendencies in science, art and politics, because it will add to the social consciousness of the time. *Mass-Observation* is not a party, a religion or a philosophy, but an elementary piece of human organization and adaptation. It is one part of a general deflection of emphasis from individual to collective effort. It is not enough in itself to ensure mass regeneration, and has no pretence to being the salvation of anybody, either spiritually or politically. It is each man's job to find his own salvation as best he can. *Mass-Observation* merely proposes to acquaint him with relevant scientific facts. It is only through knowledge about his environment that man can change it. Whatever the method of change, the knowledge is indispensable.

But the practical test of the usefulness of *Mass-Observation* is yet to come. Convincing evidence of a widespread wish to participate has already been shown by the response to the first public announcements, which were as follows:

Letter to the *New Statesman and Nation*, Jan. 2, 1937
Second letter to the *NS and N*, Jan. 30.
News-item in *News Chronicle*, Jan. 30.
Article in February Number of *Left Review*.
Article in March Number of *New Verse*.

Over a hundred offers of co-operation came in, and a high proportion of those who offered their help are now engaged in observation. Here for example is part of a letter from Scotland:

> I shall be glad to send you a full report of incidents and conversations on the 12th February. My enthusiasm for this scheme of *Mass-Observation* is daily increasing.

Here is one from Roumania:

> I am a student at the University of Cluj, having come here to work at the Ethnographical Museum and am especially interested in racial problems, and, as a sideline, witchcraft. I do not know whether your group concerns itself with the study of racial problems etc., but suggest that here is a very wide field, especially as racial propaganda has a very important influence on international affairs. In Central Europe and in Roumania more so, the whole problem of race nationality and antisemitism has a form completely different from that taken on in the West, so that many interesting and valuable ideas could be exchanged. Please send me further details of your programme and count upon me to help in any scientific research.

From Kew:

> It is a type of work which, I am certain, is urgently needed, and if I could help in any way I would be glad to do so. I have no professional qualifications in anthropology or psychology-only a keen interest and scrappy knowledge. Nor have I much spare time. But – such as they are – my limited services are at your disposal!

And, finally:

> As you can see I live in Wigan: although not officially a depressed area, there are ten thousand unemployed in Wigan alone (population 89,000). There ought to be ample opportunity for field-work here, more particularly in regard to the use of leisure.

As a result of this response, London and its suburbs muster over 40 Observers, while there are Observers at:

Aberdeen	Cambridge
Ayrshire	Cumberland
Birmingham	Lancs (Blackpool, Bolton,
Bucks	Liverpool, Manchester, Oldham,
Cheshire	Southport, Stockport, etc.)

NEW YORK	Kent
Norfolk	Oxford
North Ireland	RHODESIA
Edinburgh	Shropshire
FINLAND	Surrey
GOLD COAST	Sussex
Guernsey	Nottingham
Hants	North Wales
Herts	Yorkshire (Leeds, Sheffield)

To preserve the anonymity of the Observers, no names are given. Each Observer will be assigned a number for purposes of filing and identification.

The three final sections will give some idea of the ground to be covered, and how it is covered at present.

(g) *Ground Plan for Research*

Hadley Cantril, American psychologist, discusses contemporary work in the social field under the following headings, in his article 'The Social Psychology of Everyday Life' in the *Psychological Bulletin*, May 1934, pages 297–330:

Fads and Fashions
Conversations
Humour and Laughter
The Rôle of Imitation in Social Life
The Functions of Suggestion in Everyday Social Life
Crowds
Revival Meetings
The Rôle of Legends in the Formation of Attitudes
    and Conduct
Institutional Concepts
The Social Consequences of Suppressed Feelings and Emotions
Patriotism and War Enthusiasm
Gossip and Rumour
Religious Cures
'There's Safety in Numbers'
Friendships
Leadership
The Relation of Custom to Good Taste and Common
    Sense

Companionship afforded by Inanimate Objects
Clothing
Popularity of Racy Movies, Stories and Newspaper Articles
Comparison of the Traits, Interests and Physical Appearance of Married Couples
Comparison of the Traits and Interests of Children with Those of Their Parents
The Nature of Attitudes
The Effect of Various Types of Social Stimuli on Attitudes
Attitudes of Different Social Classes on Heredity
The Relation of Economic Values to Public Opinion
Attitudes towards Different Races
Newspapers
Language
The Effects of Vocation on Personality Characteristics
The Nature and Function of Social Competition
Youth Movements
Popular Interest in Scientific Discoveries or Formulations
Spiritualistic Seances
The Relation of the Homogeneity or Heterogeneity of a Society to Its Advancement and to Its Acceptance of New Forms of Social or Political Control
The Psychology of Revolution
Industrial Psychology
The Psychology of Radio
Psychological Effects of Unemployment

This list raises many perspectives for research but in most cases it is hard to see how a useful survey could well be made without a greater number of Observers than have been employed hitherto. No small group of specialists could make an objective research on such questions as 'Companionship afforded by Inanimate Objects' if they merely examined such examples as came to their personal notice. For inquiries of this type, *Mass-Observation* offers immediately improved facilities.

In *Middletown*, the Lynds's classical study of an American town, six headings are put forward as covering all the things that people do there:

Getting a living
Making a home
Training the young
Using leisure in various forms of play, art, etc.
Engaging in religious activities
Engaging in community activities

A more elaborate system of headings is provided by the Plan of Anthropological Study in *Notes and Queries on Anthropology* 5th Ed. London 1929. (6s.), a textbook well worth acquiring.

The main subdivisions are as follows:

1. Physical Anthropology (i.e. measuring of skulls, etc.)
2. Cultural Anthropology
    (a) Sociology
    (b) Material Culture
    (c) Arts and Sciences
    (d) Nature Lore
    (e) Language
    (f) Archaeology

Physical Anthropology is not our immediate concern, though we shall readily co-operate with specialists, to whom our mass method may be useful. Similar reservations apply to Language and Archaeology, though such subjects as slang and the impulse to preserve ancient monuments are clearly within our scope. Material Culture, Arts and Sciences and Nature Lore (including Seasons, Calendar, Weather, Stars, Geography, Plant and Animal Lore, Natural History of Man, Medicine, etc.) overlap with our field, but the most relevant headings for us are those given under Sociology.

The chief ones are:

SOCIAL GROUPINGS

LOCAL GROUPS — Social surveys have studied many aspects of these three points

DEMOGRAPHY (VITAL STATISTICS)

THE FAMILY
  Family life
  Status of members of the family
  Status of children
  Adoption
  Adoption of adults
  Fostering

THE RELATIONSHIP SYSTEM
  Kinship grouping: classificatory systems
  Behaviour between relatives
  Duties and privileges
  Relatives by marriage

CLAN ORGANISATION
TOTEMISM
  Sub-totems
  Guardian spirit, personal totem, etc.
  Sex patron, animal brethren, sex totemism

AGE GRADES
  Organisation
  Ceremonial, initiation into higher grades, etc.
  Function-educational, military, religious, social, etc.

SOCIAL GATHERINGS
RULES OF HOSPITALITY
LIFE HISTORY OF THE INDIVIDUAL
  Daily Life
    Daily routine
    Customs and Etiquette
      ('difficult to describe fully for the very reason that they are so constantly in evidence.' Notes and Queries, p. 64)
    Salutations
    Forms of address
    Titles and precedence
    Politeness
    Meals, festivities, drunkenness
    Standards of decency
  Birth
    Birth
    Infanticide
    Abortion
    Contraception
    Physiological paternity
  Names
  Education
  General
    Physical training
    Mental training
    Moral training
    Professional training
  Puberty and initiation
  Marriage and relations between the sexes
    Premarital relations
    Conditions of marriage
      Laws regulating marriage
      Prohibition
      Incest
      Legalised incestuous marriages
      Exogamy, endogamy, etc.
      Injunctions to marry certain relations
    Forms of Marriage
      Residence and place of cohabitation
      Monogamy
      Polygamy
      Polyandry
    Supplementary unions
    Preliminaries to marriage
      Age of marriage
      Defloration
      Betrothal

- Elopement
- Marriage by exchange
- Women taken under hostile conditions
- Marriage with dowry or bride-price
- Divorce
- Adultery

Ritual union and ritual continence
- Prostitution
- Marriage with the dead
- Marriage to inanimate objects
- Marriage to gods
- Symbols of coitus
- Marriage ceremonies
- Seasons far marriage
- Tree marriage

The status of women
Sexual anomalies
Abnormalities
- Impotence
- Sterility
- Frigidity
- Homosexuality, etc.
- Unmarried persons

Death and the disposal of the dead
- Beliefs concerning death and the dead
- Causes of death; spirits, sins, physical
- Spirit; soul stuff
- The fate of the spirit
- The other world
- Reincarnation

Treatment of the dying and dead
- Treatment before the disposal of the body
- Preparation and disposal of the body
- Inhumation or interment
- Cremation, etc.
- Encasing the body
- Exhumation
- Grave goods
- Treatment of property
- Burial places, ossuaries, mourning, etc.
- Ceremonies preceding disposal
- Funeral feasts
- Sacrifices
- Mourning
- Shrines, memorials and resting places of the dead
- Abnormal deaths
- Suicide
- Treatment of the enemy dead

ECONOMIC LIFE
ECONOMICS OF THE SOCIAL GROUP
COLLECTING, HUNTING AND FISHING
AGRICULTURAL LIFE
- The cultivators
- The land
- Labour
- Produce

PASTORAL LIFE
SOCIAL FRAMEWORK
PRODUCTION AND DISTRIBUTION
- Production
- Division of labour
- Stimuli to work
- Motives in work
- Economic magic
- Distribution

OWNERSHIP AND CONSUMPTION OF WEALTH
TRADE, EXCHANGE AND CURRENCY

REGULATION OF PUBLIC LIFE
   Political institutions
      Chieftainship and kingship
      Councils
      Magicians
      Rank
      Slavery
      Secret societies
   Law and justice
      Sanctions (social reactions to the action of the individual)
      Justice
      Property
      Land tenure
      Inheritance
WARFARE
   Causes and occasions of war
   Truces and treaties of peace
   Customs of war
   Organization of warfare
   Naval expeditions
PRIMITIVE MENTALITY
DREAMS
RELIGION AND MAGIC
   Magico-religious beliefs.
   Mythology
   Stock explanations
   Minor rites and beliefs
   Terminology
   Animism
   Totemism
   Spirit helpers
   Cult of the dead
   Hero-cult
   Rite, prayer, spell, incantation, etc.
   Sacrifice
   Taboo

These headings appear in a schema drawn up by committees including A. C. Haddon, Henry Balfour, C. G. Seligman, Sir Arthur Keith, J. L. Myres, H. Peake, T. A. Joyce, R. R. Marrett, with advice from J. H. Driberg, B. Malinowski, Audry Richards, etc., and approved by the British Association for the Advancement of Science, 1929. The schema assumes that it is only to be used on persons referred to throughout as primitives uncivilized, natives or savages. Nowhere is it suggested that anything of the sort is in any way applicable to ourselves. Some of it is obviously not directly applicable. But some of the least obviously applicable headings gain significance when we correlate phenomena observed at the present time with their origins and the historical changes that have modified them.

Such a framework as this will be most useful to us as a starting point. As we proceed it will be developed, modified and supplemented until it becomes unrecognizable. It is a framework which has worked with fair success among 'natives' and is the fruit of experience and study by many great men. We must use their experience, remembering that the framework was not designed for our purpose. We shall not rest content with its excellent categories.

A single section of it, such as 'Behaviour between relatives' could be made by *Mass-Observation* the subject of exhaustive research. The advance over so wide a field must be planned and co-ordinated at every step and must at the same time be sufficiently elastic to modify itself in accordance with our accumulating experience. Each batch of results will provide the possibility of technical improvements and will bring to the surface further problems for research.

Finally here is a mixed list of possible topics of inquiry, sent in by many different Observers:

Reactions for and against vaccination
Antisemitism
Funerals and undertaking
Behaviour at war memorials
Sophistication and class
'Flu epidemics
Quick and slow walkers
Punctuality of visitors
Effect of aeroplanes, especially when flying low
Contents of shop windows
Litter on streets
Use made of street crossings
Smoking. Note when people start smoking; what were they speaking about when they produced cigarettes
Secret societies
Childbirth and female problems
Depilation
Cultural significance of the indoor plant
Gestures and shouts of motorists
Telephone behaviour
Class distribution of etiquette

This list is representative of the Observers' response when the idea of observing everyday life first got home. Since those early suggestions, there has been growing up a more detailed collective understanding of the nature of the total inquiry.

The Ground Plan for Research will evolve gradually out of suggestions and counter-suggestions both by untrained Observer and scientific expert.

(h) Organizations with similar aims

These are the ones known to us. We apologize to others that may have been omitted, and hope to hear from them.

INSTITUTE OF SOCIAL RESEARCH. Carries on most of its activities in U.S.A. Until recently attached to University of Frankfurt; now functions as a separate institute in Geneva, Paris and London. Publishes *Zeitschrift für Sozialforschung*, with basic idea that 'to-day Sociology can develop only in the closest relationship with a number of other sciences, especially with Economics, Psychology, History, and philosophy. The materialistic trend in European philosophy is here formulated in a way which is in accordance with the present state of knowledge, and application of modern problems.

Since the essentials of the criticism of idealism are extensively included in this formulation, this view may constitute a powerful instrument for the whole science of Sociology.' Anthropology is not included among the list of relevant subjects. In association with Chapman and Hall Ltd. there is published a library of Modern Sociologists, the acting editors being A. F. Wells and Dr J. Rumney, who supplied this information.

FOLK-LORE SOCIETY. Deal only with obvious relics of the past, with the unusual and not with the ordinary. They have most interesting and valuable data of this sort, including dialect material.

INSTITUTE OF SOCIOLOGY, 35 Gordon Square, London W.C. Declared objects: 'To promote the study and teaching of sociology: the sociological study of human communities: the use of sociology in education: the application of sociological studies to urban and rural development.'

Most important activity is the making of maps of a region by fieldwork. Parties are sent to Gascony, Ross-on-Wye, etc., who study the geology, biology, geography, anthropology, psychology, archaeology, history, art, language, industry, social conditions and public administration of the district. Fifty of such surveys have been carried out. A piece of work has been done on St. Pancras, studying the flora of the open spaces, the pubs, cinemas, housing estates, etc.

ST. ANDREWS UNIVERSITY GROUP. Dr O. A. Oeser of the Department of Psychology at St. Andrews has organized a team of psychologists, sociologists, economists, who have devoted themselves to a study of, so far, method in the first place, the clarification of concepts in social psychology in the second. Dr Oeser believes that 'social psychology and anthropology ought to be together – one is essential to the other.' The group's first publication was in April 1937, *British Journal of Psychology*.

SOCIAL PSYCHOLOGISTS' GROUP. A group of scientists at Cambridge and London Universities who have for the past eighteen months been working on questions of method in relation to Social Anthropology.

EDINBURGH GROUP OF PHYSICAL ANTHROPOLOGISTS. Have been working on measurements of people in Scotland for the last two years. Robert Kerr, of the Royal Scottish Museum, and Prof Rose of St. Andrews are concerned.

PECKHAM HEALTH CENTRE. St. Mary's Road, Peckham. At first sight, a social club. Large modern building, with swimming bath, gymnasium, etc. The real centre of the place, however, is the laboratory and doctors' room. The Centre admits to membership local families (the unit) on payment of 1s. per week per family and on condition that each member goes through a thorough medical examination on entering. Present membership about 450 families, rising satisfactorily after a life of two years. Object is to study health and behaviour 'in a free environment'.

Political and Economic Planning (P.E.P.). Started in 1931 through the fusion of several informal small groups which had been independently interested in industry and distribution, in the social services and in national reconstruction generally. It now includes more than a dozen working groups, with headquarters at 16 St. Anne's Gate, S.W.1. In the words of a manifesto, few of its members are active partisans of any political party. A professional, fact-finding and socially responsible attitude is the one thing that members have in common. The exploration of the wider issues behind their everyday jobs and the breaking down of water-tight compartments are their common objectives. They are working towards an objective, rapid, planned development of policy, as distinct from a continuance of haphazard and conflicting expedients, on the one hand or of abrupt and brutal departure from tradition on the other. P.E.P. does not go in for an ambitious platform or press campaigns, appealing for mass support.

PEP is hardly concerned with the mass of people, though this mass is concerned with the subjects of the researches. The PEP reports emphasize mechanical and economic efficiency especially in terms of the combine. But they have collated a great deal of data in an intelligent way. The PEP publication Planning for 24 March 1936 gives a good summary of scope and technique.

INDUSTRIAL WELFARE SOCIETY: 'was founded in 1918 to encourage firms to develop such voluntary activities as affect the safety, health, security and social wellbeing of their work-people.... During nearly twenty years of existence it has drawn on the experience of many thousands of firms, and has thus built up a store of authoritative information which is not elsewhere available' (from the Society's brochure). Membership is open to firms and individuals interested in any way in the Society's objects. Advice is given to members on Health, Accident Prevention, Legal Questions, Recreation, Canteens, Appointments, Employment (personnel records, education, training, and promotion schemes, incentives and labour turnover problems). Chairman of Council is Sir Charles Craven (Vickers Armstrong Ltd.). Others include Major Astor, M.P., Sir Josiah Stamp, Viscount Wakefield and a number of Trade Union leaders.

NATIONAL INSTITUTE OF INDUSTRIAL PSYCHOLOGY. Really a firm of consulting psychologists, who send their representatives to other business firms with the object of overhauling their use of human labour. They charge fees for these overhauls, and claim to increase output, smoothness and efficiency. Also give consultations to public school boys with a view to putting them into suitable careers. Do research on problems such as rhythm in typing, etc. On the Council are among others: Sir T. Barlow, Sir W. Beveridge, Sir W. Citrine, Sir Robert Hadfield, Frank Hodges, Lord Melchett, Air Vice-Marshal Sir D. Munro, Cyril Burt, F. C. Bartlett. Finance is raised by subscription. Among subscribers are I.C.I., Bank of England, Boots, Iron and Steel Federation, Standard Telephones and Cables, Kodak, Rolls Royce, Harrods, Cadbury, etc.

NATIONAL COUNCIL FOR MENTAL HYGIENE. Chandos House, Palmer St., S.W. This is in brief the psychiatrist movement. Among the declared objects are: 'The improvement of the mental health of the community, involving a closer and more critical study of the social habits, industrial life and environments of the people.' Also 'To secure an important position for psychiatry in the medical curriculum.' Committee consists almost entirely of doctors and includes Buzzard, Horder, Dawson of Penn and the Bishop of London. Membership: doctors and lay people interested in psychiatry. Methods of work, to give lectures, have discussions, interest local authorities, act as centre for the whole movement.

(i) Some relevant literature

Important work has been published in America, especially in a series issued by the University of Chicago Press; and also in Germany. Among a great many that are relevant, the following books are outstanding:

Park, R. E., Burgess, E. W., and McKenzie, R. D. *The City*. Chicago. 1925
McKenzie, R. D. The *Neighbourhood*. Chicago. 1923
Galpin, C. J. *Rural Life*. New York. 1918
Lynd, R. S. and H. M. *Middletown*. London. 1929
Lazarsfeld-Jahoda, M., and H. Zeisl. *Die Arbeitslosen van Marienthal*. Leipzig. 1933
Ratzel, F. In '*Die Grosstadt*' Dresden. 1903
Bakke, A. *The Unemployed Man*. London. 1933
Boas, F. *Anthropology and Modern Life*. London. 1929
Wells, A. F. *The Local Social Survey in Great Britain*. London. 1935
Wells, H. G. *The Idea for a World Encyclopædia*. Edinburgh. 1937

BACK COVER

This Pamphlet is the first issued by *MASS-OBSERVATION*; it describes the aims, methods and work of this new organisation, which sets out to accomplish sociological research of the first importance, and which has hitherto never been attempted: namely, to collect a mass of data based upon practical observation, on the everyday life of all types of people: and to use the data for scientific study of Twentieth-Century Man in all his different environments.

Professor Julian Huxley in his Foreword stresses the current need for research of this kind and says 'the Technique of *Mass-Observation*, here set forth by the inventors, seems to me of great value.... I commend this pamphlet to the attention of the intelligent public, and I hope that out of it big things will grow.'

MASS-OBSERVATION needs the co-operation of all kinds of people. It already has observers all over the country: but many more are needed. All can be of assistance, and anyone wishing to become a Mass-Observer should send a postcard to:

MASS-OBSERVATION
6 GROTE'S BUILDINGS, S.E.3

Notes

1. James Frazer, *The Golden Bough: A Study of Magic and Religion* (Auckland: Floating Press, 2009. 1890), 410.
2. Readers of the original would have recognized this description as Imperial Brand Player's Navy-Cut Cigarettes. The image of the sailor and sea was first used in 1883, with the lifebuoy added five years later. Imperial tried numerous looks for the sailor, nicknamed 'Hero', until in 1927, they settled on a standardized image. Together with the alliterative and memorable saying, 'Player's Please', Imperial's brand marketing was hugely successful. See Matthew Hilton, *Smoking in Popular British Culture, 1800–2000: Perfect Pleasures* (Manchester: MUP, 2000), 100–4.
3. I alone have the key to this wild parade.
4. The British Library has created an excellent online resource that catalogues and discusses 'the UK's rich landscape of regional accents and dialects': https://www.bl.uk/british-accents-and-dialects/ (accessed 29 January 2022).
5. Robert S. Lynd and Helen M. Lynd, *Middletown: A Study in Contemporary American Culture* (New York, NY: Harcourt Brace, 1929). The Lynds's study focused on Muncie, Indiana. Marie Jahoda, Paul F. Lazarsfeld, and Hans Zeisel, *Marienthal: The Sociography of an Unemployed Community* (1933). Both studies inspired Harrisson's Worktown project, though Jahoda and Lazarfeld's work more closely resembled Harrisson's work in Bolton: the investigators acted as participants, not observers, employing an 'open-ended approach, the opportunistic use of whatever research methods came to hand, [and] the juxtaposition of quantitative and qualitative data'. Hinton, *Mass Observers*, 79–80.
6. A memory game using cards or objects developed in the 1920s by the Pelman Institute.
7. This emphasis on recruiting civilians as Observers stands in direct contrast to state monitoring of public and private life and opinion that existed in one party authoritarian regimes like Nazi Germany, and serves to underscore the democratic element of Mass Observation. For Nazi monitoring, see Claudia Koonz, *The Nazi Conscience* (Cambridge, MA: Belknap Press, 2003), chapter 4.

3

Uncivilizing sociology: How Mass Observation can free the discipline

Rachel Hurdley

Introduction

Five young men come in together at 9.42, and drink with abandon, ordering ahead of their requirements... .First round first man finishes in two minutes, and the next round he takes five minutes... the ringleader of the group shouts out, 'You bet I can sup that bugger!'[1]

There is a multitude of sociological research publications drawing on Mass Observation (MO) as a substantive resource, and debating how sociology, along with many other disciplines, has been influenced by the eclectic methodologies of MO's founders. The history of MO, its turn to public surveying, demise and resurrection are also widely reviewed across disciplines. Its mixed, even contradictory methods and methodologies have been discussed and debated for decades. Research into diaries of individual Mass Observers demonstrates the growing interest in ordinary lives, writing and histories. The chapter starts with a brief summary of key MO writing. It then pulls out five strands of MO's characteristics to consider how these might influence current sociology. First, I discuss the physical archive and its digital companion, followed by the complex sociality of this early social science. Next, the depth and breadth of MO, and multimodal approaches of both the 'directors' of MO and volunteer reporters, are considered. Last, the chapter will debate the MO broader aim of democratizing and politicizing culture, from a king's coronation to a pub round. This, I argue, is the principal legacy of MO, and vital for 'uncivilizing' sociology.

Since Angus Calder's ground-breaking use of MO material in *The People's War*, many researchers have turned to MO.[2] As Liz Stanley comments, 'Its history is entwined in complex and fascinating ways with the history of the disciplines of anthropology, economics and particularly with sociology'.[3] Theoretical and methodological issues in using the Mass Observation Archive have been discussed since the early years of its resurgence in the 1980s as the Mass Observation Panel.[4] For an excellent overview of these in the twentieth century, see Dorothy Sheridan.[5] For a history of MO, James Hinton's book is a comprehensive study.[6] Nick Hubble traces the MO's early intellectual development.[7] The early years of MO have long been seen as important in the history of sociology.[8]

I focus mainly on the early years of MO, before the Second World War, to gauge how MO's early, even utopian aims, can influence twenty-first-century sociology. The detailed interrogation of everyday life 'fully to penetrate the society we were studying, to live in it as effective members of it and percolate into every tiny corner of every day and every night of industrial life'[9] is a key definition of an 'anthropology of ourselves', or 'anthropology at home'.[10] As both observers and observed, 'ordinary people' wrote in a way that encompassed the personal and the social. This resonates with Charles Wright Mills's sociological imagination as 'the vivid awareness of the relationship between personal experience and the wider society' enabling us to 'grasp history and biography and the relations between the two within society'.[11] A focus on ambiguous and unsettled ordinariness, like the 'everyday', is an important contribution MO made to multiple disciplines, as was the decision to focus on behaviour rather than what people wrote or said in response to statistical surveys.[12] Tom Harrisson wrote of surveys, 'Among thousands of figures, there nowhere appears the figure of a man'.[13] He criticized them for representing only attitudes rather than behaviour. Key to understanding MO as more than a 'mass of unrelated facts' is to recognize the methodology underlying observation. Observers were recording everyday behaviour: 'No question of social habit or social groups were in their minds when they wrote, so that we can see these factors arising quite spontaneously'.[14]

As this chapter will show, MO's influence has been profound, in the disciplines of Social History, Cultural Studies and Social Sciences. Sociologists who have encountered the Archive, either as 'secondary' data or through commissioning Directives, recognize its refusal to fit into neat data boxes or to allow tidy narrative disseminations. Its contents, forms and methodologies burst out of books, files and folders like Jack-in-the-Boxes. The chapter focuses on the broad potential for MO to influence current sociology. Its aim is to show how MO can accomplish this, in the practice of research: the focus on practices rather than theory and in the focal variation from the long view to mid-range and close up that its methods achieved. The interplay between collective and individual practices, observation of others and of oneself and the plurality of methods offer diversity, contrast, even contradiction and failure. This is at odds with grant funding regimes demanding guaranteed findings, knowledge contributions and outputs. Yet MO continues to thrive, to fascinate and enrich multiple disciplines. It is in this enlivening, sometimes chaotic and always multi-faceted character that sociology as a discipline can find renewed vigour.

A note on editing: the chapter is organized according to the editorial technique of Humphrey Jennings, which is discussed in the section, 'The Multimodal Prism'.[15] Rather than explain and analyse the excerpts heading each section, these are set in juxtaposition to what follows, to be read in context with the sections, and with other header extracts from early Mass Observers. Similarly, images punctuate the text without written interpretation. Just as the piano player, on being asked what she had just played meant, played it again, images are a different mode of representation and meaning from text.[16]

Materiality: Analogue/digital artefact

[Harrisson] sifted through the evidence in the MO files and has turned them into what he thinks should be their interpretation rather than what their true interpretation is.[17]

No archived collection, organized in digital or physical files, is 'pure'. In this section, the eclectic, sensory materiality of the physical Mass Observation Archive is discussed, and its complex relations with the digitized sections of MO. As the chapter is written for sociologists, who may, like me, have limited experience of many archives, unlike historians or archivists, this section is for the near-novice. Before reading this book, the reader would gain so much by first visiting the Archive at The Keep in Brighton, Sussex. Doing this, as well as browsing the digitized sections online, and reading the many papers and books drawing on or reflecting on MO makes the discussions, dilemmas and arguments real. If MO remain in the abstract sphere, rather than manifest as the tangible relics that live in those folders and boxes, its material presence can never be appreciated. My first visit as a very serious doctoral student disturbed my orderly thesis, upset its textbook methodology and transformed both its aesthetic and the monograph that followed.[18] Subsequent visits over twenty years have led to annoyance, captivation, confusion and delightful excursions into other lives, times and places. Conferences, seminars and exhibitions speak to the fascination and potential MO offers to multiple disciplines and arts practices. To hold it at arm's length as a collection of datasets for analysis would be both misguided and reductive.[19] Further, a deep appreciation of cultural and historical contexts, and a recognition that MO is never finished is critical to using it. This rejection of 'snapshot' research and of tidy conclusiveness is well-put in Sheridan's refusal of the 'treasure trove' approach to the Mass Observation Archive.[20] Such an anatomical approach, cutting out interesting quotations from the mass of writing and images, detaches such sections from the social practices that are central to MO, both in the observations and in the practices of observation themselves.

Entering The Keep brings researchers into the bulky, laborious world of paper, often imperfectly filed by previous visitors. Rust stains, tears and ink spots remind us to treat these materials gently, as fragile artefacts made and handled by other people. We are never alone with 'data'. Life drawings are scattered amid lists of philosophers and scribbled addresses. Letters appear, with comments, amid other types of document. Such varied textures, interruptions, marginalia and absent presences demand attentiveness and care, from the forms of text/image to the materials and media used.[21] Only pencils are made available at The Keep for making our own paper records. Researchers can now take photographs, which serve to emphasize the aesthetics of representation, transforming writing to image. Vulnerabilities, of materials, of their human makers and handlers, are tangible, unlike the immaculate appearance of screen-mediated documents. Visitors can choose to use a tablet or laptop, rather than pencil or paper, or to view the extensive digitized MO records available online.

These approaches may appear to tame the complex materiality of the Archive. However, as Lucy Robinson argues with regard to her own project, *Observing the 80s*, the digital is not an 'exact copy' of the physical archive, but produces a 'cross-pollination'.[22] Thus, the twin digital and analogue productions encourage us to consider the relations between the humane physicality of the archive and its digital presence, between the differing hierarchies and connections within these manifestations and the institutions that created them. The different affordances of text, image and sound that Robinson's project put together also resonate with the texts and images of the Mass Observation Archive. Her digital archive had a deliberated lack of searchable 'key words', preventing decontextualization and reorganization of the digital order. This apparent limitation leads us to question how the physical Archive materials are related to each other. To request a particular document, the visitor must use an online system to find a file within the listed hierarchies. Three may be selected at any one time, which itself can lead to odd juxtapositions. Documents are gathered in paper folders, but selecting the desired document often means finding it gathered with other documents; a notebook is in a folder with other notebooks, press cuttings and pamphlets; a photograph is in a box with a hundred others, sorted into envelopes. This too produces chance connections, much in the way that the MO founders intended the 'shock' of juxtaposition in the 12th May compilation. The organization, therefore, of documents or files within the online filing system, within the physical folders, and in relation to the other two documents or files requested is not just subject to archivists' decisions in file organization online and offline, but also researchers' sequential selections of required materials, three at a time, which sometimes leads to new themes and pathways.

The varied media used in the Archive and at other sites, such as Bolton Museum and online: photographs, drawings, paintings (oil and watercolour), collage, hand, typed and digital writing, as well as film and audio, have their own implications in the 'politics of identity, form and representation'.[23] The

Image 1 *Drawing of dresser, ca. 1938. Worktown Collection, Observations in Bolton. SxMOA 1/5/18/57/B/3. University of Sussex Special Collections: Mass Observation Archive.*

materiality of the archive not only has impact on the digital, but also *vice versa*. The ability to search for terms online brings up, for example, 'king' in multiple instances, producing a complete, albeit over-complete thematic collection (since it will bring up the names of pubs and so on). The very completeness of such a search only emphasizes the near-impossibility of repeating this in the analogue Archive. However, the power relations change; as a researcher, I can no longer perform a quick search of the term I want, but will come across it in many different folders, in very different contexts. This possibly democratizes the process of research, in denying the researcher an omnipresence. Both analogue and digital can offer complete collections of whatever the researcher wants, but the methods and organization differ. Awareness of gaps, frictions and alignments between the two Archives makes visible what is missing: the non-Observers, the unsent diaries and blurred photographs, for example. As Masashi Hoshino comments, 'We need to imagine what may be lost, and then recognize that all we will ever be able to do is imagine it, because we will never know'.[24] Social memory thus becomes entangled with the sociological imagination; we fill in the gaps with our own assumptions and cultural understandings. MO therefore politicizes processes of organization and selection of sociological data. Through making researchers aware of omissions and absences, of the need to follow pre-ordained search and selection methods and of how these produce particular organizations of research objects, MO highlights how knowledge and meanings are produced. Paradoxically, through offering so much, the Archive forces researchers to sharpen the knife cutting out the boundaries of the research field. This in turn illuminates the *a priori* anatomy of knowledge that precedes conventional research project designs.

Foregrounding of the politics of knowledge is evident in the historian, Carolyn Steedman's, theorization of Dust (as material and philosophy) and the Archive, for 'our understanding of *how things happened*, indeed, is bound up with this understanding: that there is sequence, event, movement; things fall away, are abandoned, get lost…. Dust – the philosophy of Dust – speaks of the opposite of waste and dispersal; of a grand circularity, of nothing ever, ever going away'.[25] As the counter of 'waste', Dust contains everything, makes possible a narrative of anything, but, especially for historians, makes it impossible to impose an 'end', but rather an 'ending', of a series of endings in which everything is, eventually rolled up at some unknown future end of history. So much is there in the Mass Observation Archive that might be disposed of in a carefully designed research project, with aims, objectives and well-defined research questions. Confusion, annoyance and diversion through the by-ways of MO hierarchies, folders and files forces the researcher to reconsider how she wastes so much in the eagerness to make a thesis, an 'end'. Taking a messier approach to sociological knowledge-making as a process of beginnings and endings, rather than a finite product radically alters the politics of research.[26] No longer are 'we', the academics, in charge. Rather, the participants and all the knowledge they make, even the lost and unknown have presence. We know that anything we do not use in a publication is still there, for discovery and reuse.

For sociologists, the distinction between 'using' and 'reusing' data has led to considerable debate.[27] A turn to history, avoiding what David Inglis called 'presentism', is a methodology sociologists can take from MO.[28] What MO facilitates is allowing traces and trails through decades and within chosen moments to emerge, borrowing from contemporary historical methodology. Presentism in current sociology is partly a side-effect of funding regimes and publication pressures. MO is unique in its combination of diaries and day surveys, Directive reports and in its 1980s reincarnation, the Mass Observation Panel, affording opportunities for reflection on and revisiting of early topics and methods. While snapshot sociology – a slice through a moment of history – is sometimes all that is possible in a research project, making explicit this a-historicism is the least we can do.

Archivists and historians working with archives 'play their parts in a political drama, and a politicised history', requiring them to 'look at rather than through documentation'.[29] Employing historiography in their research contextualizes their work, critically engaging with the documents and media of history-making and an awareness that research 'findings' can be no more than partial accounts of an endlessly deferred 'truth'. This suggests that sociologists can also recognize the politics of recording and representation as well as analysis. This resonates with MO founders' original aims, in collecting as much material from as many Observers as possible, to produce a democratic reportage of Britain, rather than the top-down, survey-based academic analyses that dominated social science. MO's many publications had to be edited, but do contain multiple Observer accounts. Comparing MO books with what is available in the Archive, and making similar selections for contemporary research disseminations, emphasizes the difficulty of editing. Making explicit the politics of publishing research, the knowledge of what and who are left out, as MO's founders did, conserves their 'utopian impulse'.[30] The hope is always there that, somehow, research representation will become democratic.

Complex sociality

Tom, of course, has been sweet as sugar at this end, possibly because he may suspect that you must have written to me, I don't know. Anyway, he mentioned you today without showing any signs of animosity. But that's just like him, the shit.[31]

MO was not a stand-alone research project. For example, Humphrey Spender was brother of the poet Stephen Spender and thus connected with his poetry circle. Madge brought with him the experience and networks of Fleet Street. Harrisson was influenced by his ornithological background, and Bolton's appeal was that, being the birthplace of William Lever, it was symbolically connected with 'cannibal' life in Melanesia through Unilever's global market.[32] The Chicago School of Sociology and other US ethnographic/fieldwork endeavours guided its methodology. Bolton was chosen as Worktown partly because Arthur Bowley, professor of statistics at the London School of Economics, had carried out two statistical studies in Bolton and other industrial towns earlier in the century, and this suggests that MO's founders were aware of 'mainstream' academia, refracting its findings through its own lens. Humphrey Jennings 'was learning under John Grierson, in the GPO Film Unit, the skills which would make him Britain's most distinguished documentary film director'.[33] The film *Spare Time* is a collage, or montage, of the 'Leisure' observations, extended by Jennings into the steel, cotton and coal communities of Sheffield, Manchester and Pontypridd.[34] It is an exemplar of the long workshop of MO, how it extended its influence into the future work of its 1940s and 1950s funders, as well as being influenced by multiple fields of practice and theory. This is a reminder to bring all of our networks, histories, influences and knowledges into play when doing research, and to be explicit about this. The inner circle of 1930s Observers was sometimes gossipy, sometimes backbiting and frequently communicating their feelings about other members of the group. This section aims, first, to contextualize MO social science within the social. Second, it debates the complex, happenstance, often surreal sociality of this social science. Arguing in smoky rooms, watching seaside crowds; calling on vicars and drawing churches. Bodies fighting other bodies at wrestling matches and sheltering from bombs in underground train stations. Two painters back-to-back on a rooftop; exhibition visitors seeing themselves on display; Observers being observed. Mass and noise, small talk and letters. Finally, beyond these contemporaneous encounters are those that occur over the decades and across disciplines.

The embodied, sensory and often forced sociality of Bolton observers, both in the house at Davenport Street and in the field, is vividly conveyed by Humphrey Spender's recollection:

> At our disgusting breakfasts in the smelly parlour of our headquarters house, Tom Harrisson would talk me into taking my camera to christenings, Holy Communions, pubs, railway stations, public lavatories. Away from headquarters I was very much on my own, sometimes, frightened, embarrassed, bored and depressed. To the working people of this town my manner of speaking was la de fucking da. To me their language and accent was foreign.[35]

Contrast this with a letter to Tom from Henry Novy, 27 February 1940, from 85 Davenport Street, Bolton:

> This last week we have been hard at work trying to collect material for the special area report. By now I know quite a lot of people, most of them through interviewing house to house […] [W]e are now on very good terms with about 50 housewives… who told us we were welcome anytime. I have had long talks with many of them, which I enjoyed and found quite enlightening on conditions I had only heard of. I sacrificed most of my time to the task of making friends, and took very few notes. […] Concentrating on the people and making them the center [sic] of interest. I can't over-emphasise the enthusiasm I have for this work.[36]

These opposing, yet intimate views of the social, interactive aspect of *doing* research, exhibit the ongoing reflexivity of observers. A rare photograph of a woman at her scullery sink illustrates just how Spender integrated himself, despite his fear and embarrassment. At the time, photographs of working class domestic interiors were unusual. Perhaps the only notable exemplars can be found in the Foundations of Sociology/Sociological Review Archive, kept at Keele University library. However, these were taken for a very different purpose, relating to social work in Chester. For Spender to have gained such access suggests he established a good rapport with this individual. His photographs of what was usually invisible to the public eye are particularly striking, such as the image of children playing on wasteland (image 2).

This integration of Mass Observers, particularly those making images, is shown by Michael Wickham painting in the streets and Julian Trevelyan making collages. As Wickham says, 'the idea being that we would get public comments and you would actually have a relationship between the artist and the people'.[37] Had twenty-first-century researchers seen only these photographs, without Spender's reflections on his acute feelings of alienness and depression,

Image 2 *'Children play on wasteland near Gray St.'* Humphrey Spender 1938. © Bolton Council. From the collection of Bolton Museum.

they would see only the product, rather than the process. It takes time to become immersed in the field, and can be painful. Writing field notes that include reflections on this experiential process, and making the decision to include extracts of these, as well as formal methods, is invaluable for novice researchers, who can take these accounts into the field with them, knowing that they are not the only ones to find doing research difficult. This processual methodology is not always explicit, as in the case of the diarists. While each of these may be seen as individuals writing alone, they nevertheless were in processes of interaction with other accounts, as, 'while responding to directions from MO, [they] also interpreted these prompts in their own ways and to suit their own needs. This could be true even when they paid close attention to the wider MO project – reading its publications, and following press coverage'.[38] In these different 'social' scenarios, we can see MO opening up to the unknown, to possibilities and mundane serendipity rather than tightly planned project design, despite Harrisson and Madge's apparent control over the themes and questions. Participants move beyond the remit.

An exhibition in Bolton of photographs and other materials relating to the Worktown study in 1978 was not simply a matter of visitors consuming the spectacle. They commented on, corrected and named people and places in the photographs.³⁹ They also commented on previous entries, in a kind of ongoing conversation, making jokes and political points. Children visited and commented on the photographs, even though they themselves had no memories of the people or events, thus bringing the past into the present, linking 1930s and 1970s childhoods. Dorothy Sheridan recalls 'feeling quite moved' following her talk in Bolton, during another exhibition in 1993.⁴⁰ The emotional, affective dimensions of sociality come across in these encounters.

Conversations between researchers and the 'researched' in the Archive continue, during what is never a linear, one-way data-gathering pursuit, but an ongoing dialogue with the Mass Observation Archive, that becomes richer as understanding of MO grows. Even when a Directive is specifically commissioned by an academic, it is near-impossible to limit oneself to that Directive, since the Reports that come back are unlike any conventional data. Louise Purbrick writes, of the 1999 Directive she commissioned on wedding presents: 'The effect of this seven year long period of reading and re-reading is that I feel as if I have been engaged in a dialogue with Mass-Observation correspondents. It has certainly not been a straightforward information gathering exercise … Analysis is not the exclusive preserve of academics and Mass-Observation correspondents, like most people, have their own ideas.'⁴¹ Thus, MO challenges any notion of a top-down research project, from the data collected, to analysis. Purbrick's reflections also convey the benefits of doing slow sociology.

The following are notes I made in The Keep after reading the contents of a folder. The content matters, but also the fact that I made the notes. Like Robinson, Purbrick and other MO researchers, I was in a conversation with the Observers, in parallel with what I was reading:

> What comes through in these letters is the back and forth of mailed correspondence, missed calls, not getting hold of people, money concerns, Tom Harrisson flying out of the country, the Travellers Club (his hangout), complicated negotiations about copyright, ownership, photos, text etc..... Also, the way in which people's characters, voices, relationships with each other come across, the 'presence' of what's happening as they write, or shortly before writing, where they are (from headed paper or handwritten addresses), the back and forth between institutions, companies, individuals, with lots of handwritten addenda on letters and added notes.⁴²

The exchanges I noted, and others, read like a modernist, fragmented epistolary novel. The battle for money from Harrisson, the alleged promiscuity of one Observer and relationship problems of another, the difficult personality of a Davenport Street inhabitant, efforts to publicise findings, the different localities and embodied experiences of these sites are portrayed not through decontextualized description but through communications from one person to another. Relationships emerge from these exchanges too, while the addenda and notes convey the process of doing things, rather than completed accomplishments. Evident too is the passage of time, so different from the swiftness of today's communications. Also, slow research, even using 'snail mail', allows time for thoughts to settle, for ideas to be added and the original left too, on paper, rather than being too quick to delete, edit and leave only the revision. Perhaps there is something to be learnt here, of observing how we communicate with others, not just with research participants, but also wider circles, including students, archivists, other researchers and project collaborators during and after a project.[43]

Finally, returning to the very first Directive on Mantelpieces in 1937 for new Mass Observers, we can see how dialogues continue back and forth across the decades and beyond the academic sphere.[44] This first Directive prompted David Pocock to repeat the exercise in 1983, and the current MO team to send out a third Mantelpiece Directive in 2019.[45] These resonate with each other, and within the three separate collections of respondents' Reports. Not only analysed in research publications, they have been discussed on radio, in online conversations and conferences.[46] In response to these, people have tweeted photographs of their mantelpieces.

Richard Slee's 2020–2 'Mantelpiece Observations' exhibition, displayed in several UK museums, drew on the 1937 Mass Observation Mantelpiece Reports and Humphrey Spender's Worktown photographs.[47] Slee's ceramics are enlarged, fantastically surreal interpretations of display artefacts hosted on abstracted wooden mantel-type units, in rooms where his selection of Spender images are hung on the walls. Moreover, the bare mantelpieces of Hove museum itself, where the work has been exhibited, offer a visual echo of Slee's 'mantelpieces'. Schoolchildren were invited to respond to the exhibition by making their own mini-mantelpieces; YouTube films are available of Slee talking about thinking and making the objects. A collaboration between Bolton Museum, the Mass Observation Archive and the Museum of the Home was inspired by Slee's exhibition. 'A Little Festival of Mantelpieces' brought artists, filmmakers, writers and academics together (in online events, due to Covid).[48]

Thus, sociability can be seen throughout twenty-first-century MO events. Conferences and seminars and exhibitions are held, which are cross-disciplinary and non-disciplinary, since the Observers themselves, retired academics who continue their interest in MO and interested members of the public (including children) attend. In the pressure to publish, sociology (and other disciplines)

Images 3, 4, and 5 *Three photos of Slee Mantelpieces. Credit: Richard Slee: Mantelpiece Observations exhibition, Bolton Museum, 2020. Photo by Joel Fildes.* © Bolton Council. From the collection of Bolton Museum.

tend towards producing academic outputs, or 'Impact' through engagement with policy makers. 'Engagement' is a secondary consideration, but it is through engaging with other people throughout the research process that sociology enters the public realm. Public sociology is what makes it relevant to non-academics, who are not just 'lay audiences', but active citizens.

Latitude and longitude

We have been called: maniacs, organisers of a cult, crankly, beastly, Groupey… Mass-Mystics, spies, Nosey Parkers, Peeping Toms, lopers, doodlers, snoopers, envelope steamers, little boys bird's nesting, keyhole artists, sex-maniacs, Sissies, Society playboys, and (Ah!) human beings.[49]

Depth of detail and chronological breadth within the Mass Observation Archive are the dual and related foci in this section. As vertical and horizontal axes, these provide syntactic and paratactic possibilities for understanding the grammar, or structure, of society. Of great value are the long view, and oscillation between big ideas and mundanities of everyday life, examples of which we have seen in previous sections. The Directive responses, the May 12th day diaries, individual diaries and the input of paid Observers, for example, offer multiple intersections of biography and history. Hubble calls the diarists 'agents of history', despite their apparent task to write the details of their personal lives; their very role as MO correspondents 'gave them the confidence to pronounce on public matters with an authority they would not otherwise have had in a hierarchical society'.[50] There is a dual vision in correspondents' writing, which is evident even today, writing in the present as if it were already in the past. As Trevelyan wrote, 'We liked to think that it was forming a museum for future generations of social historians'.[51]

The depth of detail, from lists of hats worn in a pub, to minute-by-minute accounts of drinking sessions, day diaries from waking to sleeping, drawings, film and photographs of dancing, collections of press cuttings, pamphlets and event programmes is a salutary lesson in 'immersion' into 'every tiny corner' of social life.[52] The diversity of accounts means that, 'For better or for worse, we can only insist that *every* generalization about forty million Britons is endlessly subject to qualification ... This account tries to preserve the marvel of that human variety, although to have played it down would have made it much easier to draw conclusions with impressive sweep'.[53] In the same book, *Living through the Blitz*, Harrisson writes about revisiting the war diarists in 1972/3, asking them to write about the same experiences, but this time from memory, what he calls the 'double take'. Accounts from memory are recoloured with unity, with the '"magnificent"' and '"splendid"' public attitudes and behaviour and the '"enchantment"' of '"glossifying"' history.[54] An example is a girl in Stepney who, in her wartime account, is playing the piano, misses Chamberlain's speech and the first siren. Thirty years later, she 'completely transforms those events in memory' to one of the whole family sitting around the wireless and the first siren leaving her '"shaken to the roots"', and it turns out she has been recounting her transformed memory for decades.[55] The sociology of memory therefore has much to take from MO's longitudinal aspect, as does academic interest in nostalgia.

The horizontal was underpinned by a commitment to recording 'ordinary' lives. For instance, in a call for volunteers and donations, there is the prediction that the history of 'ordinary citizens' will be as important, if not more so, than military and political histories.⁵⁶ This is justified by citing Tolstoy's *War and Peace*: 'To study the laws of history, we must completely change the subject of our observation, must leave aside kings, ministers and generals and study the common, infinitesimally small elements by which the masses are moved'.⁵⁷ Micro-practices shape the patterns and rhythms of life, making sense of ordinary, ongoing 'history'. In the same way, macro-sociology and a growing emphasis on Big Data can only provide a fraction of sociological knowledge. Nor can sociology of élites account for the cultures and practices of everyday life.

Yet, reflection on the novel revelations of ordinary lives was sometimes tempered with disillusionment, as in Julian Trevelyan's letter to Dorothy Sheridan about a book that Harrisson had planned on art before his death in 1976. The Ashington Group were miners in Northumberland, who had taken classes with the Workers' Educational Association [WEA], and whose work was widely exhibited. This 'Unprofessional Painting', as Harrisson and Trevelyan called their exhibition, was an element in the 1930s excitement over working class amateur art.

It is notable that the Ashington Group did not consider themselves in this light; an example of the balance between objectivity and subjectivity in 'Mass

Image 6 *Jimmy Floyd, Pigeon Crees, c. 1938 Ashington Group*. By kind permission of the Ashington Group Trustees.

Observation' tipping towards objectification of the observed. This can be seen in Trevelyan's comments nearly four decades later in the letter:

> It is curious that, although the group still goes on, with younger chaps, it has become the antithesis of what Tom thought it. He concieved [sic] it as working class people, their own lives, with an admiring audience around them, now they lead rather a life apart, and they have no effect in the community. At that time we all encouraged everyone to paint, but now the world is full of mostly rather bad amateur painters, and they need discouragement if anything.[58]

Does Trevelyan make a good case for discouraging the democratization of art practice, which is used as a method in social research? Probably not, but his point about the loss of community art practice is salient. Art does not belong only in galleries, nor should it be only a professional practice. Just as MO was about the practices or methods of doing research, in amateur social groups and/or alone, art is as much about process as product. Moreover, to treat paintings only as things to be observed is counter to the MO's inherent dual vision, of objectivity and subjectivity, observation and self-reflection. What comes across here is the difficulty of maintaining that duality, of not imposing top-down classifications. At its best, MO defies simplistic typologies of social groups and practices, encouraging further interrogation of modern-day categorizations.

The long life of MO allows for the long view, in an ongoing reconsideration of the past and the present. Three approaches to using MO for longitudinal research illustrate this. Emma Casey combines two MO directives on gambling with other research to excellent effect, to question modern-day attitudes towards women gambling.[59] Bill Bytheway takes two sets of MO Reports from 1990 and 2002, with 120 people contributing to both, to analyse how 'this reflects their unfolding experience and changing feelings about age'.[60] Third, Hubble *et al.* combine MO with University of the Third Age [U3A] members' accounts, giving the study both breadth and depth to challenge modern-day assumptions on ageing.[61] Analysing not only the content, but also considering MO form and methodology is an aspect of these studies.[62] Using (or 're-using') MO material necessarily leads to methodological reflexivity, and also to rejecting quantitative methods, as Harrisson did.[63] Attending to form, not only of data but also of research questions, is vital for valid analysis. Closed survey questions, with tick-box responses and perhaps a last qualitative question for 'colour', cannot do justice to participants' forms of response, of narrative or other forms, and also the ways in which they might inflect research questions. 'Findings' are always open to reinterpretation, as Jennie Taylor and Simon

Prince undertake, arguing that 'the pub study's archive contains material that goes against the published findings'.[64] As researchers, we might not want to invite secondary use of 'our' data. However, for validity, this is crucial. Critiques of analyses add to our sociological understanding. Finally, how researchers are observed as subjects by the 'subjects' of research matters, further emphasizing the need to exercise reflexivity.

The multimodal prism

I wonder how high the pile is of letters and M.O. diaries I've written. I bet it would surprise me. I always longed to be clever and write books. I bet I've written a few in the shape of letters and endless scribbles![65]

Here, the multimodal approaches of both the directors of MO and volunteer reporters are considered. Multimodality is a nascent methodology in sociology, contested and subject to constant innovation, without tempered reflection on what has already been practised in the early years of the discipline. The prismatic concept 'mass observation' offers multiple affordances through refraction, reflection and polarization. 'We shall collaborate in building up museums of sound, smell, food, clothes, domestic objects, advertisements, newspapers, etc.' claimed the founders.[66] Reporters submit lists, essays, reflections on 'mass observation' and self, drawings, photographs, diagrams, day surveys, reports and diaries. These are echoed in the many modern representations of MO materials, including the edited diary series of Nella Last and television film, popular history books such as David Kynaston's and exhibitions at Bolton Museum and Art Gallery.[67] Such careful selections lend coherence and completeness, in contradiction to what Humphrey Spender calls, 'this great principle of never fixing anything'.[68] This section examines how the great mass of different theories, media, forms, styles and textures could, nevertheless, come together to make some kind of sense.

Trevelyan's watercolours for the Worktown project brought painterliness to the project, together with William Coldstream's differing style. The visual dimensions of their paintings, other sketches and Spender's photographs also juxtapose with written lists, descriptions, letters and ideas. Like Spender, Trevelyan's surrealist aesthetic, in his collages and famous suitcase, expanded upon the founders' interest in this movement, towards the 'shock' of juxtaposition and uncovering of the 'mass unconscious'. Harrisson wanted Coldstream and

Image 7 *'Washing day near Snowden St. Park Mill is visible in the background.'* Humphrey Spender 1938. © Bolton Council. From the collection of Bolton Museum.

Graham Bell's 'severe realism' as well as Trevelyan and Michael Wickham's surrealism and impressionism, telling them: 'It is because we distrust the value of mere words that we are keen to employ artists and photographers.'[69]

Yet Trevelyan's MO watercolours contrast with his contemporaneous oil paintings of the Potteries, which he saw as a resistance against Harrisson's imposition of style and subject. This sometimes uneasy collaboration led to a heady mix of surrealism and documentary, poetry and reportage; collections of cultural artefacts: flyers, press cuttings, postcards, brochures, even 'candy rock and the themes of popular music hall songs and jokes' to encompass 'real life'.[70] Later, they collected what Harrisson calls the 'documentary story of the war, in posters and postcards, wrappers and pamphlets, menus and bills, programmes, Christmas cards, war books, popular tunes, film scripts, sermons and public speeches'.[71] Material culture was not just pictured and described, it was collected.

Julian Trevelyan writes: 'I was applying the collage techniques I had learnt from the Surrealists to the thing seen, and now tore up pictures of the Coronation crowds to make the cobblestones of Brighton. [...] [I]t was a legitimate way, I think, of inviting the god of Chance to lend a hand in painting my picture.' Returning to London from Bolton, Trevelyan lingered to paint the Pottery towns in oil, building on his experiences and techniques in Bolton: 'I put away my suitcase of collage scraps and returned to oils and brushes.'[72] Like Coldstream and Bell, he had become accustomed to producing images on the spot, from direct observation.

The visuality of MO is present not simply in the paintings of Bell and Coldstream; the paintings, collages and photographs of Trevelyan; the drawings of Walter Hood; Spender's photographs and Jennings's widely known film, *Spare Time*.[73] Lucy Curzon considers Jennings's philosophical stance: 'As Jennings states, images – none of them isolated, rather "each is in a particular place in an unrolling film" ... [it] is in these acts of metamorphosis or potential for creation that the image's revolutionary potential, in part, resides.'[74] We can see this in Jennings's compilation for *May the Twelfth*, for which he was principally responsible. Combining Observers' Reports, responses to questionnaire leaflets and mobile Observers' accounts in London, he likens his technique for editing the day of George VI's coronation to using a camera for different 'kinds of focus... close-up and long-shot, detail and ensemble'.[75] Thus, the visual is not merely a method of observation, but a methodology. Just as a film is edited to produce meaning, or photographic publication is arranged to convey, for example, a narrative, montage or thematic interpretation, *May the Twelfth* uses organization and juxtaposition to transform the meanings of individual extracts through the power of the mass. In other words, the selection and editorial techniques, based on a visual methodology, is the analysis.

The influences of documentary film-making and surrealism, 'twin but, as it turned out, *contradictory* impulses' were clear from the outset.[76] *Spare Time* which combines film from Bolton with film from Manchester, Sheffield and Pontypridd, is a film of under 15 minutes that conveys and widens findings from Bolton, justifying what was drafted for the Worktown project.[77] In collection and representation techniques, surrealism and documentary influences are apparent. The poetic character of MO, a kind of metaphysics in which realism and surrealism, autobiography and writing 'the other' come together in the alchemy of representation is a methodology, however seemingly contrary, that sociologists can bring to their own work. While Stanley conceives these as contradictory, as have other scholars, some argue otherwise, such as Tyrus Miller, who considers that, 'formally innovative experimentalism and naturalistic explorations of everyday life were not so much opposed as instead *complementary* moments of a broader modernist poetics'.[78] Somehow, the cacophony, contradictions, even failures of MO entwine, or resonate, or rub

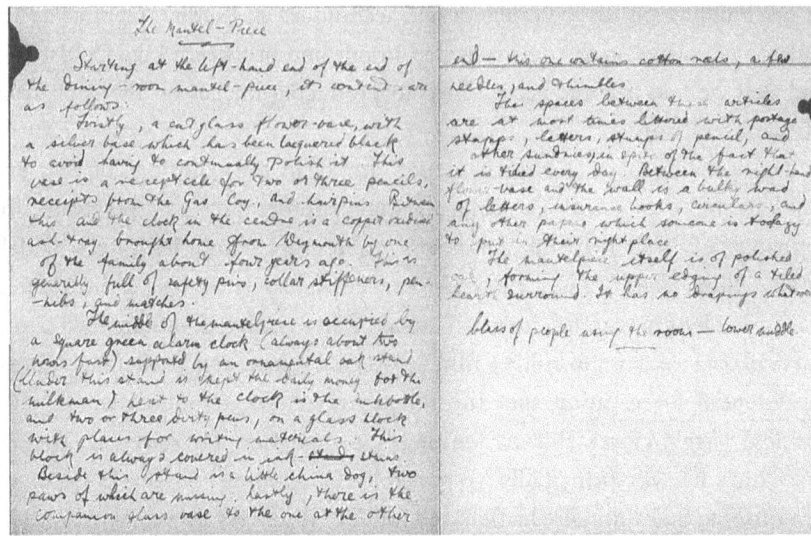

Image 8 *June 1937 Day Survey Mantelpiece Reports, D. Nicholson, Schoolboys' Reports. SxMOA 1/3/7/3: University of Sussex Special Collections: Mass Observation Archive.*

Image 9 *C1154, Autumn 1983 directive SxMOA 2/1/13/1/4. University of Sussex Special Collections: Mass Observation Archive.*

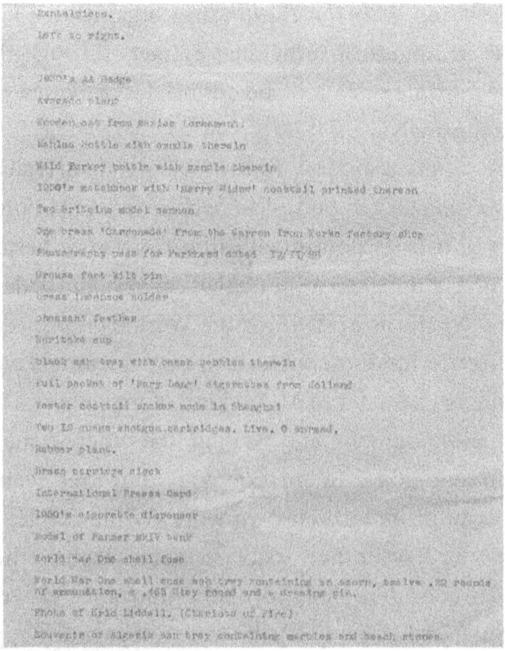

up together to make sense, in contrast to the common sense of conventional assumptions.[79]

Political public sociology

I felt the queerness of a system that carefully preserved its property by painting it frequently and thought not at all of the health of its human work people. Preservation of woodwork. Ruination of employee's health [...] To know that every little piecer dislikes the life he leads at work, and to see how conditioned he has to become, he curses, rails and dreams, but he comes up every day for more. For more bad air. For more slow painful hours. For meagre wages. After work is over he jumps into a round of pleasure.[80]

MO promises hope; it was based on ambition, willingness to experiment and fail, humanizing argument and gossip, and a commitment to democratizing how knowledge was made and how it was represented, for and by self and society. We can see the roots of Cultural Studies in MO. Writing about 'Cultural Studies and radical popular education' as 'resources of hope', Tom Steele states, 'The most rewarding popular education form is… one based on dialogue and "conscientisation" where, in a collective situation, students get to understand how the multiple languages of oppression function and learn confidence in their own expression'.[81] Oppression is both observed and experienced in the writings and images of MO. These not only raise Observers' self-awareness, but also educate the reader without this being a deliberated outcome.

Leisure is politicized; descriptions of holidays in Blackpool, or gambling and drunkenness do not portray the 'fecklessness' of the working classes. These are necessary counterpoints to the pathology of capitalist exploitation. This fits within, but also challenges left-wing understandings of the 1930s and 1940s. MO made culture relative, individualized and detailed, denying a single working-class culture. 'M-O's findings were politically troubling [...] It corrected the impressionistic valorisations of working-class culture which were otherwise commonplace in the Popular Front-era left.[82] Watching and walking are economic ways of spending the holiday, as Gary Cross points out. The following by a Bolton worker holidaying in Blackpool is an example of implicitly politicized, seemingly trivial writing that conveys the experience of the culture/economy intersection:

I took the kiddies on the pleasure beach but I was a bit disappointed there as to have a ride it would have cost me 6d. and 3d. each; and to have had two or three rides for all of us, well it would have cost me a little too much; but anyway we enjoyed ourselves all the same watching other people spending money.[83]

To subvert intellectual interpretations of 'the working-class', MO not only made active citizens and autodidacts of its Observers, but also, through publications, countered popular assumptions and what was seen as falsifying mainstream reports of the rise of Fascism. This was more than conveying information; such education was an essential for a functioning democracy. As such, MO presented a challenge to the institutions of government and the press, where the 'facts' of social inequality and threats to democracy were either ignored or misrepresented.[84]

MO's pursuit of public, uninstitutionalized and disruptive knowledge-making and learning has a philosophical connection to the early days public adult education, as espoused by the WEA. Indeed, MO observed WEA and other adult education classes in Bolton in 1937. It encompasses what Raymond Williams later theorized: that 'culture is ordinary'. As argued earlier in the chapter, 'ordinary' is neither fixed nor apolitical; it is a contested and mobile term, politicizing the taken-for-granted everyday.[85] In particular, his notion that 'the process of society as itself a process of education' resonates with MO.[86] Williams calls the elite educators '"Old Humanists"',

> guardians of a process by which elite culture defined society's values and norms. However, he regarded the Old Humanists as already losing their influence to the new 'Industrial Trainers', harbingers of an economic and social order based on mass production and mass consumption for which new technical skills were demanded from the education system.[87]

MO promotes the opposite both of elite, institutionalized social science and of the more recent technocratic skills-based 'industrial training'. Correspondents were and are free to respond to Directives as they choose, to write in their diaries how they wish. The 1937 Coronation was not the history of a king being crowned, but of boredom, excitement, tea and cigarettes, rubbish and paper hats. No top-down formal pomp, nor the drudgery of writing for the purpose of improving 'skills': MO's aim was not to improve research skills, nor to act as an improving influence on the masses. Education is a social process, produced by the mass for the mass. Note that this is not 'the masses' of political and economic theory, which, in that powerless, disenfranchised plural, separates those masses from the élite. We are all the mass, a collective that assembles knowledge through continual practice of observation and reflection.

Conclusion: Uncivilizing sociology

The real issues of sociology can only be addressed if the sociologist is prepared to plunge deeply under the surface of British life and become directly acquainted with the mass of people who left school before they were 15... The issues cannot be fully viewed by statistical interviewing, the formal questionnaire, and the compilation of data on the library level.[88]

One of MO's most notable characteristics is that it could be seen as a failure in today's pressured academic environment, and was seen as a poor cousin to institutional academic sociology even at its birth. Casey *et al.* discuss the historical reasons for MO's negative reception within the nascent discipline of sociology.[89] The first Mass Observers were honest about their failures: as Sheridan writes, 'Humphrey Spender gets thrown out of a pub for taking photographs... Walter Hood chats up the subject of his research... young male observers are teased by millgirls... Penelope Barlow... gets invited for tea'.[90] 'Chaotic, disorganised and lacking in focus it may have appeared, but it was the chaos that comes from vision and high aspiration on a shoestring.'[91] In the twenty-first century, meaning-making, in particular, how sociological knowledge is made, who makes it, and how it is represented, too often depends on disciplinary consensus for funding and peer review. An important attribute of MO is its multi- or non-disciplinarity. Its diffuse origins, popularity as a social historical resource and for Cultural Studies, encourage working across boundaries, offering 'methodological opportunities'.[92]

Research design can be overly prescriptive, data collection confined by pre-emptive decisions about what is 'out there', and analysis limited by the use of software programmes. The MO method, at times seemingly bizarre and random in its focus, was deliberately so. As Spender comments, although aware 'of the whole thing described for example by Orwell, but not wanting to allow myself to know too much about it', a purposeful ignorance of what was being observed is, even now, a desirable attribute for doing bottom-up research. Talking about his newspaper work, Spender criticises '*The Mirror*'s policy... of framing up, rather dishonest'.[93] This methodology, of openness in observation and representation, counters current demands in terms of fixing research questions, interview schedules and survey questions. Canonized forms of research representation, especially writing conventions, desiccate the richest of projects. MO's surrealist, visual and poetic roots blow these conventions away. Kathleen Raine wrote that for Madge, 'who seemed a man inspired almost as a medium is inspired or possessed, the idea of Mass Observation was less Sociology, than a kind of poetry, akin to surrealism'.[94]

Surrealism is not just a stylistic device, and nor is poetry. MO's visionary zeal is linked to its strongly visual and surrealist methodology.[95] Just as classical economic theory is now being challenged by behavioural economics, rationalist sociological theory is undermined by MO. 'M-O was to break through the profoundly mythologised rationalisation of everyday life – its systematic representation in scholarship (from Weber on) as well as in the mass media as a sphere of disenchanted, rationally calculated behaviour, purged of phantom, fetish and spirit.'[96]

The chapter has considered how MO's characteristics might influence current sociology. First, how its analogue and digital manifestations politicize processes of selection and organization, followed by the dialogic, social and networked character of the ongoing practices of Observers, researchers and others. Next, the longitude and latitude of MO, both palimpsest and panorama, not only facilitates longitudinal research projects, but also promotes a processual and open analytic methodology. The multimodal approaches of MO, particularly the strongly visual methodology underpinning techniques of representation, and the realist/surrealist interplay undermine 'common sense' methods of data collection, analysis and representation. Last, I argued that its public, political and progressive impulse is the principal legacy of MO.

Although sociologists have written of MO's effects on their approaches, particularly in historiographic, dialogic, messy methodologies, MO offers more. The founders' vision of a democratic social science, as both social research and social movement, presents a compelling future for sociology as a politicized, public endeavour of active citizens and engaged academics. Having discovered a letter he wrote from his time in Melanesia, Tom Harrisson comments, 'Reading this letter I get an uncanny Bristley [sic] feeling. It proves to me what I have often doubted – that I do know what I'm doing'. In the earlier letter itself, an 'extraordinary document', he writes, 'I shall study uncivilization, as the key to humanity & sense – & myself [added in pencil]'.[97] In pursuing this, MO was deeply unsettling to the *status quo*, to the conduct of civilized and civilizing discourse. It is my hope that today's sociology will do the same, with curiosity and a sense of both the magic and struggle of everyday life.

Notes

1   Tom Harrisson, *The Pub and the People: A Worktown Study* (London: Gollancz, 1943), 180.
2   Angus Calder, *The People's War: Britain, 1939–45* (London: Jonathan Cape 1969).

3   Liz Stanley, 'Archaeology of a Mass Observation Project', *Manchester Sociology Occasional Papers* no. 27 (1990) (Manchester: Department of Sociology, University of Manchester), 1.
4   David Bloome, Dorothy Sheridan and Brian Street, 'Theoretical and Methodological Issues in Researching the Mass-Observation Archive', *Mass Observation Archive Occasional Paper* no.1 (1993), University of Sussex Special Collections: Mass Observation Archive.
5   Dorothy Sheridan, 'Reviewing Mass-Observation: The Archive and Its Researchers Thirty Years on', *Forum Qualitative Sozialforschung / Forum: Qualitative Social Research* 1, no. 3 (2000): Art.26.
6   James Hinton, *The Mass Observers: A History, 1937–1949* (Oxford: Oxford University Press, 2013). See also *Speak for Yourself: A Mass-Observation Anthology 1937–1949*, edited by Dorothy Sheridan and Angus Calder (London: Jonathan Cape, 1985).
7   Nick Hubble, *Mass Observation and Everyday Life: Culture, History, Theory*, 2nd edition (Basingstoke: Palgrave Macmillan, 2010).
8   Angus Calder, 'Mass-Observation, 1937–1949', in *Essays on the History of British Sociological Research*, ed. Martin Bulmer (Cambridge: Cambridge University Press, 1985), 121–36.
9   Tom Harrisson, 'Preface', in *The Pub and the People: A Worktown Study*. Reprint (1943; London: Faber and Faber, 2009), 6.
10 Tom Harrisson, Humphrey Jennings and Charles Madge, 'Anthropology at Home', *New Statesman and Nation* (30 January 1937): 155.
11 Charles Wright Mills, *The Sociological Imagination* (Oxford: Oxford University Press, 1959), 6.
12 Claire Langhamer, '"Who the Hell Are Ordinary People?" Ordinariness as a Category of Historical Analysis', *Transactions of the Royal Historical Society* 28 (2018): 175–95.
13 Tom Harrisson, 'The Future of Sociology', *Pilot Papers* II, no. 1 (1947): 10–25. SxMOA1/1/12/4/7, University of Sussex Special Collections: Mass Observation Archive, 11.
14 Charles Madge and Tom Harrisson, eds., *Mass Observation: First Year's Work*. Reprint (1938; London: Faber and Faber, 2009), 9.
15 Charles Madge and Humphrey Jennings, eds., *May the Twelfth: Mass-Observation Day-Surveys by over Two Hundred Observers*. Reprint (1937; London: Faber and Faber, 2009), 90.
16 Rachel Hurdley, 'Focal Points: Framing Material Culture and Visual Data', *Qualitative Research* 7, no. 3 (2007): 355–74.
17 Humphrey Spender, SxMOA32/117/2&3 (University of Sussex Special Collections: Mass Observation Archive, 1977).
18 Rachel Hurdley, *Home, Materiality, Memory and Belonging: Keeping Culture* (Basingstoke: Palgrave Macmillan, 2013).

19 Annebella Pollen, 'Research Methodology in Mass Observation, Past and Present: "Scientifically, about as Valuable as a Chimpanzee's Tea Party at the Zoo"?', *History Workshop Journal* 75 (2013): 213–35.
20 Dorothy Sheridan, 'Damned Anecdotes and Dangerous Confabulations: Mass-Observation as Life History', *Mass-Observation Archive Occasional Paper* no. 7 (University of Sussex Special Collections: Mass Observation Archive 1996), 1.
21 Ben Kafka, 'Paperwork: The State of the Discipline', *Book History* 12 (2009): 340–53.
22 Lucy Robinson, 'Collaboration in, Collaboration out: The Eighties in the Age of Digital Reproduction', *Cultural and Social History* 13, no. 3 (2016): 403–23, 419.
23 Rebecca Wright, 'Typewriting Mass Observation Online: Media Imprints on the Digital Archive', *History Workshop Journal* 87 (Spring 2019): 118–38, 119.
24 Masashi Hoshino, 'Humphrey Jennings's "Film Fables": Democracy and Image in the Silent Village', *Modernist Cultures* 15, no. 2 (2020): 133–54, 138.
25 Carolyn Steedman, *Dust: The Archive and Cultural History* (Manchester: Manchester University Press, 2001), 166
26 Niamh Moore, '(Re)Using Qualitative Data?', *Sociological Research Online* 12, no. 3 (2007):1–13.
27 Moore, '(Re)Using Qualitative Data?', 1–13; Mike Savage, 'Revisiting Classic Qualitative Studies', *Historical Social Research/Historische Sozialforschung* 30, no. 1 (2005): 118–39.
28 David Inglis, 'What Is Worth Defending in Sociology Today? Presentism, Historical Vision and the Uses of Sociology', *Cultural Sociology* 8, no. 1 (2014): 99–118.
29 Terry Cook, 'The Archive(s) Is a Foreign Country: Historians, Archivists, and the Changing Archival Landscape', *The American Archivist*, 74, no. 2 (2011): 600–32, 631–2.
30 Hoshino, 'Humphrey Jennings's "Film Fables": Democracy and Image in the Silent Village', 138.
31 Letter from Brian Barefoot in London to Henry Novy in Bolton, February 1, 1940: SxMOA37/1/5/29. University of Sussex Special Collections: Mass Observation Archive.
32 Tom Harrisson, *Britain Revisited* (London: Gollancz, 1961), 25.
33 Calder, 'Mass-Observation, 1937–1949', 121.
34 Humphrey Jennings, *Spare Time* (UK: GPO Film Unit, 1939).
35 Humphrey Spender, *Lensman: Photographs 1932–52* (London: Chatto and Windus, 1987), 15.
36 Letter from Henry Novy to Tom Harrisson, 27th Feb 1940: SxMOA37/1/5/29. University of Sussex Special Collections: Mass Observation Archive.
37 Cited in David Hall, *Work Town: The Astonishing Story of the 1930s Project That Launched Mass-Observation* (London: Orion, 2016), 101.

38 Timothy Ashplant, '"Subjective Cameras": Authorship, Form, and Interpretation of Mass Observation Life Writings', *The European Journal of Life Writing* (2021) 10: MO16-MO44, MO19.
39 SxMOA32/117/1. University of Sussex Special Collections: Mass Observation Archive.
40 SxMOA32/117/1. University of Sussex Special Collections: Mass Observation Archive.
41 Louise Purbrick, *The Wedding Present: Domestic Life beyond Consumption* (London: Routledge, 2007).
42 SxMOA32/117/5. University of Sussex Special Collections: Mass Observation Archive.
43 Robinson, 'Collaboration in, Collaboration out: The Eighties in the Age of Digital Reproduction', 403–23.
44 Mass Observation, 'Mantelpiece Directive'. University of Sussex Special Collections: Mass Observation Archive, 1937.
45 Mass Observation, 'Autumn Directive'. University of Sussex Special Collections: Mass Observation Archive, 1983; Mass Observation, 'Winter Directive'. University of Sussex Special Collections: Mass Observation Archive, 2019.
46 Hurdley, *Home, Materiality, Memory and Belonging: Keeping Culture*. Rachel Hurdley, 'Synthetic Sociology and the "Long Workshop": How Mass Observation Ruined Meta-methodology', *Sociological Research Online* 19, no. 3 (2014): 177–202.
47 Richard Slee, 'Mantelpiece Observations' (Ceramics Exhibition, 2020).
48 Bolton Museums, 'A Little Festival of Mantelpieces', 2020.
49 Charles Madge and Tom Harrison, *First Year's Work: 1937–1938* (London: Lyndsay Drummond, 1938), 63.
50 Nick Hubble, 'Review of Mass Observation Online', *Reviews in History* 969 (2010a): n. pag.
51 From Julian Trevelyan, *Indigo Days*, 2nd edition (1957; London: Scholar Press, 1996), cited in Dorothy Sheridan, 'Appendix', in *The Pub and the People*, 2nd edition (London: Cresset, 1987), 351.
52 Tom Harrisson, 'Preface', in *The Pub and The People* 2nd edition (Welwyn Garden City: Seven Dials Press, 1970), 6.
53 Tom Harrisson, *Living through the Blitz* (London: Penguin, 1978), 17.
54 Harrisson, *Living through the Blitz*, 326–7.
55 Harrisson, *Living through the Blitz*, 322–3.
56 *Home-Front History and Mass-Observation* [pamphlet]. SxMOA32/120/10/1. University of Sussex Special Collections: Mass Observation Archive, n.d.
57 Tolstoy, Leo, *War and Peace*, trans. Anthony Briggs (1869; Harmondsworth: Penguin, 2007), part 11, chapter 1.
58 Letter from Julian Trevelyan to Dorothy Sheridan, November 16, 1982. SxMOA32/104. University of Sussex Special Collections: Mass Observation Archive.

59 Emma Casey, *Women, Pleasure and the Gambling Experience* (London: Routledge, 2008).
60 Bill Bytheway, 'Writing about Age, Birthdays and the Passage of Time', *Ageing & Society* 29, no. 6 (2009): 883–901.
61 Nick Hubble, Jennie Taylor and Philip Tew, eds., *Growing Old with the Welfare State: Eight British Lives* (London: Bloomsbury Academic), 2019.
62 Dorothy Sheridan, 'Using the Mass-Observation Archive', in *Researching Ageing and Later Life: The Practice of Social Gerontology*, edited by Anne Jamieson and Christina R. Victor (Milton Keynes: Open University Press, 2002).
63 Mike Savage, 'Changing Social Class Identities in Post-War Britain: Perspectives from Mass-Observation', *Sociological Research Online* 12, no. 3 (2007): 14–26.
64 Jennie Taylor and Simon Prince, 'Temporalities, Ritual, and Drinking in Mass Observation's Worktown', *The Historical Journal* 64, no. 4 (2021): 1083.
65 Diarist 5353, Nella Last 21 November 1943.
66 Madge, Charles and Tom Harrisson, *Mass-Observation* this volume, 48.
67 Last, Nella, in *Nella Last's War: The Second World War Diaries of Housewife, 49*, ed. Richard Broad and Suzie Fleming; Nella Last, in *Nella Last's Peace: The Post-War Diaries Of Housewife, 49*, ed. Patricia Malcomson and Robert Malcomson (London: Profile Books, 2008); Nella Last, in *Nella Last in the 1950s*, ed. Patricia Malcomson and Robert Malcomson (London: Profile Books, 2010); Victoria Wood, *Housewife, 49*, [Film] Dir. Gavin Millar (UK: ITV, December 10, 2006); and David Kynaston, *Austerity Britain 1945–1951 (Tales of a New Jerusalem)* (London: Bloomsbury, 2008).
68 Humphrey Spender, 27/7/1977 interview with Derek Smith, SxMOA32/117/2&3. University of Sussex Special Collections: Mass Observation Archive.
69 Quoted in David Hall, *Work Town: The Astonishing Story of the 1930s Project That Launched Mass-Observation* (London: Orion, 2016), 236.
70 Cross, Gary, ed., *Worktowners at Blackpool: Mass-Observation and Popular Leisure in the 1930s* (London: Routledge 1990), 4.
71 Harrisson, 'Preface', in *The Pub and the People*, 12–13.
72 Trevelyan, *Indigo Days*, 84–5.
73 Jennings, *Spare Time*.
74 Lucy Curzon, *Mass-Observation and Visual Culture: Depicting Everyday Lives in Britain* (London: Routledge, 2017), 125. See also Boris Jardine, 'Mass-Observation, Surrealist Sociology, and the Bathos of Paperwork', *History of the Human Sciences* 31, no. 5 (2018): 52–79.
75 Madge and Jennings, eds., *May the Twelfth: Mass-Observation Day-Surveys by over Two Hundred Observers*, 90.
76 Liz Stanley, 'Mass-Observation's Fieldwork Methods', in *Handbook of Ethnography*, ed. Paul Atkinson, Amanda Coffey, Sara Delamont and John Lofland (London: Sage, 2001), 106.

77 SxMOA1/5. University of Sussex Special Collections: Mass Observation Archive.
78 Tyrus Miller, 'Documentary/Modernism: Convergence and Complementarity in the 1930s', *Modernism/Modernity* 9 (2002): 225–41, 226. See also Tanya Barson, 'Time Present and Time Past', in *Making History: Art and Documentary in Britain from 1929 to Now* [exhibition publication] (London: Tate Publishing, 2006).
79 Jardine, 'Mass-Observation, Surrealist Sociology, and the Bathos of Paperwork', 52–79.
80 Tom Binks, a side-piecer in a Bolton cotton mill, watching a painter take his time to paint the window frames, in Madge and Jennings, eds., *May the Twelfth: Mass-Observation Day-Surveys by over Two Hundred Observers*, 358.
81 Tom Steele, 'Cultural Studies and Radical Popular Education: Resources of Hope', *European Journal of Cultural Studies* 23, no. 6 (2020): 915–31, 929.
82 Alexandre Campsie, 'Mass-Observation, Left Intellectuals and the Politics of Everyday Life', *The English Historical Review* 131, no. 548 (2016): 92–121.
83 Quoted in Cross, ed., *Worktowners at Blackpool: Mass-Observation and Popular Leisure in the 1930s,* 150.
84 Tom Jeffery, [no title], *Mass Observation Occasional Papers* 1978. University of Sussex Special Collections: Mass Observation Archive.
85 Langhamer, '"Who the Hell Are Ordinary People?" Ordinariness as a Category of Historical Analysis', 175–95.
86 Raymond Williams, 'The Common Good', in *Border Country: Raymond Williams in Adult Education*, ed. John McIlroy and Sallie Westwood (Leicester: National Institute of Adult Continuing Education, 1993), 228.
87 Tim Blackman, 'Raymond Williams and the New Industrial Trainers: A Critique and a Proposal', *Oxford Review of Education* (2021): 1–15.
88 Harrisson, *The Pub and the People*, 10.
89 Emma Casey, Fiona Courage and Nick Hubble, 'Special Section Introduction: Mass Observation as Method', *Sociological Research Online* 19, no. 3 (2014):129–35.
90 Dorothy Sheridan, 'Appendix', in *The Pub and the People*, 2nd edition, 351–4 (London: Cresset, 1987), 353.
91 Hall, *Work Town: The Astonishing Story of the 1930s Project That Launched Mass-Observation*, 297.
92 Fiona Courage, 'Using the Mass Observation Project: A Case Study in the Practice of Reusing Data', *Przegląd Socjologii Jakościowej* XV, no. 1 (2019): 32–40, 32.
93 Humphrey Spender, 27/7/1977 interview with Derek Smith.
94 Quoted in Hall, *Work Town: The Astonishing Story of the 1930s Project That Launched Mass-Observation*, 46.
95 Victoria Foster, 'The Return of the Surreal: Towards a Poetic and Playful Sociology', *Qualitative Sociology Review* 15, no. 1 (2019): 148–64.

96 Michael Stewart, 'Mysteries Reside in the Humblest, Everyday Things: Collaborative Anthropology in the Digital Age', *Social Anthropology/Anthropologie Sociale* 21 (2013): 305–21, 309.
97 Tom Harrisson letter, Bolton 4/2/38: SxMOA32/120/10/1. University of Sussex Special Collections: Mass Observation Archive.

4

Voices from the archive

Jennifer J. Purcell

During the height of the Covid-19 pandemic, when nearly everyone who had a laptop and Wi-Fi was working, teaching or learning remotely, I sat down – using the online conferencing platform, Zoom – with Dorothy Sheridan, MBE, Dr Nick Stanley, and Dr Penny Summerfield, all of whom worked with Mass Observation in the 1970s and early 1980s. Much like the archival materials themselves, which remind us of the diversity of experiences, these three interviews not only provide readers with differing angles and views on the early archive and the University of Sussex, which is home to Mass-Observation and the Mass Observation Project, but also allow readers to consider the ways in which lives, careers and relationships intertwine around and through the archive, the University and Mass Observation.

As a young undergraduate at the University of Birmingham, Dr Nick Stanley crossed paths with Charles Madge, who was Head of Sociology at the time. Several years later, when Stanley happened across a reference to Mass-Observation, he remembered this connection and carried out his doctoral research on the organization, and most importantly, conducted interviews with many of the original Mass-Observers, including Madge. The resulting dissertation, *'The Extra Dimension': A Study and Assessment of the Methods Employed by Mass-Observation in Its First Period, 1937–1940*, has become an essential part of the canon of Mass Observation. After receiving his doctorate, Stanley helped to create the Gallery 33, at the Birmingham Museum and Art Gallery. This work took him, as Stanley remembers, 'back to Tom Harrisson land' in the Solomon Islands and West Papua, which would become central to the rest of his career. In the interview, Stanley remembers Madge and the interviews with Observers conducted for his research, and offers the reader a snapshot of the Archive in its early days.

Dr Penny Summerfield, Emeritus Professor of History at the University of Manchester, came to the University of Sussex as an undergraduate in the early 1970s and remembers the very early days of the archive when little had been sorted and researchers helped catalogue the material as they read it. At Sussex, Summerfield became deeply interested in researching women's history and subsequently emerged as an authoritative voice on women's experiences during the Second World War in Britain. Over the course of her career, she has developed influential theories regarding the use of oral history and the construction of personal narratives. Her account threads the archive and University into larger developments of the discipline which saw the evolution of women's history, social and cultural history, and the rise of subjectivity and self as legitimate forms of historical inquiry.

Dorothy Sheridan began as assistant to Tom Harrisson after the collection was brought to the University of Sussex in the 1970s, rebooted the project with Professor David Pocock after the death of Tom Harrisson and later became archivist of the University of Sussex Special Collections. Sheridan has edited a number of collections from the archive, including *Speak for Yourself* (with Angus Calder, 1984), *Among You Taking Notes: The Wartime Diary of Naomi Mitchison, 1939–1945* (1985) and *Wartime Women* (1990). In the interview, Sheridan remembers Sussex as an undergraduate and provides a history of the archive and the Mass Observation Project. Her account offers insight into archival management, the relationship between the archive and the observers, and underscores the influence of Mass Observation across multiple disciplines.

This is not meant to be an exhaustive study of the archive's origins at Sussex, nor an exhaustive study of the deep impacts and influences of Mass Observation since its doors opened to scholars in the 1970s – that is for another time and a much larger study. The three accounts here range across space and time, allowing us to consider the evolution of Mass Observation's legacy since its initial installation at the University and to imagine new pathways forward.

Editorial note: Unless necessary to the narrative, I have removed utterances or conversational phrases that might disrupt the flow of the narrative in the following interviews. When these expressions signify important pauses in the interview, I have included them. Additionally, I have rearranged some of the interview responses in order to knit together common subjects or themes. The full transcripts and audio interviews can be consulted at the Mass Observation Archive.

Nick Stanley

Dr Nick Stanley grew up in Birmingham and went to boarding school in Hampshire and Reading. After leaving school, spent two years in a monastery and then went to Birmingham to study Social Science. There, he met Charles Madge.

NS: [Madge] was one of the tutors in my first year. He was a kind of a shadowy figure. He didn't appear very often. He found lecturing extremely embarrassing. He wasn't a natural lecturer. Always, he was red-faced whenever he lectured. He was always very, it was excruciating being lectured to by him, because he felt so uncomfortable and you felt so uncomfortable for him. He wasn't a natural lecturer. But he didn't have to do very much. He gave us a few lectures on the Nuer and a few others on Malinowski I think, um, and that was about it.

Beyond the lecture hall, Stanley only crossed paths with Madge a handful of times during his time as an undergraduate. Richard Hoggart had recently established the Centre for Contemporary Cultural Studies in 1964, which Stuart Hall would join soon thereafter.[1] Stanley did not work with the CCCS, but he remembers a tension between the Sociology department and the group:

NS: There was a kind of a tension between what we used to call CCCS (the Centre for Contemporary Cultural Studies) and the Sociology department. There was a feeling that they were both trying to cover the same turf... The head of Sociology after Charles Madge was a guy called Gi Baldamus, who was a refugee from Germany, and was an industrial sociologist, but was also a theorist. And he was also very charismatic. And I don't think he and Stuart saw eye-to-eye. When I went on to do my masters, I went to see Stuart, to talk about what I might do. And he sort of said, 'You know I think you ought to think long and hard before you do anything in sociology', but in fact I did stay in sociology and I did my masters at Birmingham as well.

Stanley's Masters thesis was a comparison between the Community Relations Commission in Great Britain and the Northern Ireland Community Relations Commission, but while he was researching and writing his Masters project, he became intrigued by a passing reference to Mass-Observation in Donald Drew Egbert's Radical Socialism and the Arts *(Knopf, 1970). Remembering Charles Madge from his undergraduate days, Stanley decided to research Mass-Observation, reading all of the published works of the organization. Working with Janet Wolff (then at Leeds University) and Geoff Nelson from Birmingham Polytechnic, Stanley embarked on his important doctoral thesis, 'The Extra Dimension': The Study and Assessment of the Methods*

Employed by Mass-Observation in Its First Period, 1937–1940, which made a significant contribution to the 'rehabilitation of Mass Observation as a research methodology' in the 1980s.[2]

Stanley turned to the newly opened archive at Sussex to begin his research. He visiting the archive and the generosity and assistance of Dorothy Sheridan (then Wainwright).

NS: I must say Dorothy was extremely generous to me, because it was, if you think about it, letting a, letting loose a pre-doctoral student on really important material for the archive ... It was courageous and generous ... But I was left entirely free to do exactly what I wanted ... [The archive] was quite, it was quite tight. It wasn't a huge place, and there wasn't a lot of space. But it was always immensely friendly, and was always a joy to go to.

Stanley's dissertation was built upon interviews with many of the original Mass Observers, including Molly Tarrant, Dennis Chapman and Charles Madge. Periodically during his research, Stanley met with social historian, Angus Calder, who was also conducting interviews with Observers. Calder was well-known as the author of The People's War, *the seminal social history of the Second World War in Britain which drew heavily on Mass-Observation's resources prior to their being housed at the University of Sussex.*

NS: His interviews, my discussions with him, were always immensely useful, serious, provocative. I learned a huge amount from him, and he was extremely generous to me as well. And we shared our interviews, which was great really. So that I had, I think about four or five of his interviews and he had all of mine ... He was at the Open University, Scotland. At the Edinburgh base, living outside – a place called Linlithgow. And he was by that time, he was also seriously writing and his work on Mass Observation, had he finished it, would have been magisterial as was his earlier work of course ... We would meet in Birmingham. He would come to stay with me. We were able to sit in my little office and chat for hours and hours away.

Looking back, Stanley can readily call to mind most of the interviews with Observers, particularly his interview with Julian Trevelyan:

NS: One of the least successful interviews is the one I remember best, which was Julian Trevelyan, who lived in London on the Thames, on an island, which was just connected by a little bridge to the mainland. Which was an old industrial property of some kind, some kind of factory, which he turned into a house, and he lived there with his wife. The problem, I didn't discover, until about halfway into the interview was that he made his own beer, and the beer, I discovered, was extremely strong. So, by the end of the first hour things started to disappear, and I wasn't able to use my tape recorder, and my memories of it, the first half hour of it are fine and from then on, it just fades off, which is a great shame, because Julian was a great host and he got some really nice memories as well. Though in fact, both for him and for Bill Coldstream, M-O was just a change of venue, it didn't change anything about them at all, they just carried on the same. Coldstream was, I met Coldstream at UCL, with Lawrence Gowing at the time. And, we had a very 'winey' lunch, but by this time, I'd learnt my lesson. And, he got a very pinpointed visual memory, unlike Julian's, which was rather impressionistic, his was very clear, to the point, exactly where he'd been, why he was surprised by things, uh, but it didn't really change him at all. In the way that someone like Denis Chapman, it actually provided for an entirely new life for him, so there is a sense in which Mass Observation effected my interviews quite differently. And I'm not sure I was really aware of that at the time, that's why the reflection later, made me come back to think about, you know 'ah!' in that period of time how much of them has changed as well.

Coming back to the archive in the 2010s, Stanley was struck by this particular insight: might his interviewees' memories have been 'refracted' over the passage of time and across the span of a career. In a short unpublished essay entitled, 'Memories Refracted', Stanley writes, 'In 1980 it did not occur to me to reflect on how the interviewees' subsequent careers or lives might have filtered their narratives in particular ways nor how this process might become manifest.'[3] In particular, Stanley cites Dennis Chapman's interview, which Chapman began by sharing the telegram of Tom Harrisson's instructions for his Worktown observations:

I should like you to work some of the time here and in Ashington and be the moving part of the Bolton unit, if okay by you – and more interesting for you. Depends what you arrange for your family. Anyway, get to know the smells and accents of Bolton. That's the first thing. I'm looking to you to counteract the somewhat academic tendencies of Wagner and Madge, we must keep things all the time firmly rooted in the LCM of England. Spend the next four days talking to working men, cotton operatives, tannery chaps, colliers, unemployed, all over Bolton.[4]

Remembering this telegram as Professor of Sociology at Liverpool University during Nick Stanley's interview forty years later, Chapman underscored Harrisson's amateurish approach:

Now the naivety of this is that I had served a craft apprenticeship. I had spent several years selling insurance all over the county of Somerset. I came from a working class background, anyhow, and spent a year doing fieldwork in York for Rowntree with railway workers, chocolate workers, unemployed...

and here was Tom Harrisson telling me to get the sights and smells of the working class, which showed basically, how totally ignorant he was.[5]

Charles Madge, in his first interview with Stanley, reflected on the challenge of recalling the past:

> It's a very elusive business. I find it difficult to be fully truthful about, looking inside myself to know what I did, what my philosophy was at that time, because afterwards in looking back inevitably one tries to improve on the truth – to make it more convincing, more self-critical than it was in fact.[6]

Stanley spent three years tracking down his former tutor, but eventually with help from Charles Madge's daughter Vicky Randall, Stanley caught up with Madge after a lecture he had given at the University of Westminster. Stanley remembered:

NS: I heard he was going to give a talk at his daughter's department at the University of Westminster. So I turned up, and I sat through it. And, at the end, I went down – it was a big great lecture theatre – and I went down from the top to the bottom. It was only him and his daughter, Vicky Randall, there at that time – they were chatting. It was quite theatrical. I made my way down and Vicky said – oh, this is Nick Stanley. And Charles sort of crumpled. He said, 'Oh, I am sorry, I *did* mean to contact you.' And the ice was broken. But he had resolutely really refused to do it until sheer good manners made him do it.

Madge was initially reluctant to recall his links with Mass-Observation.

NS: He didn't really want anything more to do with Mass-Observation. It was a kind of link to the past that was, both painful and regretted. He never really fitted in in Birmingham. He never really took part in main academic life in the department. He was always very aloof. Running quickly to his office and one saw nothing of him, really. And, I think he probably wished that he'd done something else rather than accept the invitation from the dean of the Faculty of Commerce, Philip Sargent Florence, to become the first head of the sociology department ... It was somehow the amateurishness of it, the lack of sophistication. And although as I said, I've never heard him badmouth Tom Harrisson, ever – he's one of the very few people who I've *not* heard say something derogatory about him – I think he felt that Tom had somehow or another compromised his seriousness through the organization. And, in 1940 he was keen to be away. He missed the serious stuff, real academic business, and he was away and he never looked back.

Looking back on his own research, Stanley recognizes the challenge of making sense of Mass-Observation as an organization and its archive.

NS: Looking back on it now, it's only looking back on it now, why did I spend so much time on the statistical work? It was, I think, an attempt to try and make sense of the plethora of data, of the incommensurability of the documentation, the sense of which one can talk of it as having any kind of social science validity. So, it was a kind of a foil to my other thesis, which is about the notions about surrealism, which of course, failed. But there was this other sense in which it was about becoming statistically respectable. And that was one of the leitmotifs that went into the discussions, and the interviews, particularly with those who went on to become social scientists. How they felt about it. Whether in fact [M-O] was a crazy gypsy crusade, or whether in fact it did have something which could later become a historical document of immense importance. And I suppose statistical work actually took a huge amount of time. In those days, it was shuttle cards. Every individual that I entered had their own shuttle card. And shuttle cards went into big trays and they went to the computer centre at 8 o'clock at night, and at 12 o'clock the next day, you went to collect them and to find out where it had failed. So that it failed usually six or seven times before you could get a table out. It was very painful, and I really wonder whether it was worth the effort. I mean these days, you could do it in half an hour I suppose. It was primitive computing. Uh, and it gave me a sort of sense that I was grounded, but whether it did much more than that, I think I'll leave it for other readers to tell me.

While researching and writing his Doctorate thesis, Stanley worked in the Art Education Department at Birmingham City University.

NS: It was a department of fifteen academics and perhaps 300 students, most of them doing their teacher training to become art teachers, others coming back for masters, others coming back to do their doctoral studies, and then some quite large international projects with UNESCO International Society for Education in Art and Design [INSEA] with the British Social Science Research Council and with the Leverhulme Trust, so there was quite a lot going on. So I did my masters and then I was literally given my time to do my doctorate in my normal day. I would have a day out a week and then at weekends.

With the doctoral degree in hand, Stanley moved into BCU faculty and then on to university administration, where he then worked with the Department of Labour to employ graduate students designing ways to use anthropological artefacts from museums as teaching aids in classrooms. Here, his career path would cross that of Tom Harrisson's.[7]

NS: I worked with my local museum in Birmingham whilst we were doing this work. And in the end, I became involved in the creation of an ethnographic gallery, which actually became nationally, and to some degree internationally, quite well known, called Gallery 33, meeting place of cultures. And for that, I was sent out to the Pacific, to relook at collections – I was already looking at collections by this time – to relook at where collections were made and to make fresh collections. So this took me back to Tom Harrisson land: Solomon Islands and West Papua. I worked on and off there, in and out, with the museum, for the next few years. And then after that, I was entranced by the tale of an anthropology gallery in the middle of the jungle in West Papua… It's a place called The Museum of Culture and Progress in Agats in West Papua. People called the Asmat People. And it's known by the fact that it's where Michael Rockefeller met his end… It was extremely difficult, quite dangerous, and I discovered that it was indeed in the middle of the jungle and I spent my time working in West Papua from 1998 through till today, really.

After retirement, Stanley received a fellowship with the Museum of Art Culture, Archeology and Anthropology at Cambridge and at the British Museum. He is a member of the Department of Africa, Oceania, and the Americas at the British Museum, and Chair of the friends at Cambridge. Stanley is currently working on a chapter recalling his involvement in Gallery 33 at Birmingham Museum and Art Gallery in a forthcoming book edited by himself, Michael Rowlands and Graeme Were entitled, Reframing the ethnographic museum: histories, politics and futures, *with University College London Press.*

Penny Summerfield

Emeritus Professor of University of Manchester, Dr Penny Summerfield held an appointment at University of Lancaster as Professor of Women's History and served as Head of the School of History and Classics and Head of Arts, Histories and Cultures at Manchester. She is the author of numerous books and articles over her long career, including Histories of the Self: Personal Narratives and Historical Practice *(2018) and* Contesting Home Defence: Men, Women, and the Home Guard in Britain During the Second World War *(2007) with Corinna Peniston-Bird.*

Summerfield grew up in north London. Though many of her schoolmates went on to more traditional universities, she chose University of Sussex. Established in 1961, Sussex was the first of the new universities created after the Second World War and was known for non-traditional approaches to learning.

PS: I looked at prospectuses and I knew I wanted to do history. And a lot of places, especially the more traditional universities, basically started you in ancient history and you had to go through all of early medieval, middle medieval and late medieval, and early modern, and you more or less stopped when you got to the nineteenth century, and really, I wanted to *start* with the nineteenth century and come up as close as I could to the present, and Sussex not only offered you that, but it also offered lots of thematic courses which really caught my eye. So there were courses on revolutions and on imperialism, and it just seemed so much more exciting… And it seemed much more exciting than the traditional, sort of rather chronologically periodized history.

Sussex was very interdisciplinary, so this relates to the themes, and it didn't actually have a history department as such. It had schools of study, and history, you could take history, a history degree, in all five of the arts and social science schools of study. Now, sadly, they've gone back on that in the last, I don't know, twenty years. But when I was there, in the 1970s, you could choose your school of study, and as far as I remember, there was English and American, there was European, there was social science, there was cultural and community, there was African and Asian studies. It didn't really matter which school you were in, you could select courses from any of these, and as well as doing history courses, you had options to do philosophy, literature and what were called contextual courses, which was sort of, like one I did which was on literature, politics and society in 1930s Britain… For UK universities at that time, this sort of approach was, I think Asa Briggs called it re-writing the frontiers of knowledge. And, you know, it suited me down to the ground. It was lovely. I will say I did find Sussex a bit intimidating at first.

… Strangely enough, I'd not really experienced a campus university; I'd visited. But, living in London, going to a school in London, the idea of a campus was very new and at first I found it huge and rather impersonal and scary, and never seemed to see the same person twice, which seemed so strange, because quite quickly, by the end of the first year, I thought it was lovely. It was so beautiful, and the tall trees and the rooks nesting in them, and coming down the library stairs and all the rooks would be rising out of the trees, and the lovely sweeps and the Basil Spence architecture. Really, I found it very friendly… Also, the style of teaching, was then, kind of a small system, not that many students really. And, you had two tutorials a week, no compulsory lectures, and in your tutorial, there would be one other student. So, that's actually very, very limited contact unless you made the effort to find other people for yourself. You weren't going to find many through that sort of teaching system. That was a little bit of a challenge, you know. But, what we were expected to do was to write an essay each week for each course, so you got your head down in the library and you got on with the reading and taking notes, and getting the essay done, which suited me fine. I got into that and liked that very much.

Summerfield remembers the history faculty and history courses at Sussex in the 1970s as exciting and radical, but nonetheless still predominantly male-centred.

PS: I remember only being taught by two women in my three years as an undergrad. One was an English literature lecturer and the other was Beryl Williams, a historian. I took a course with Beryl on revolutions, where we studied the French, the Russian and the Chinese revolutions. And that was great. But it was mostly male. And, the approach to history – I was thinking about that – was kind of on a cusp. These were mostly guys who'd been educated in political history, so it was still quite political, but they also tended to be quite radical in the sense of looking for new approaches and so on. So, the kinds of history we did, we focused on, let's say, millenarian communities, the politics of Chartism, the struggle for the vote. I mean, we did that, women didn't come into it at all [laughing]. Actually, in one course, they were a tiny fraction of one week [laughing]. It just seems amazing doesn't it? But it, I mean, and then it was all about the ILP, the Independent Labour Party, and SDF, the Social Democratic Federation, and radical parties. And trade unions, so there was quite a lot of kind of labour history, which was different from elite political history, even if it still was broadly within the mould of political history. These contextual courses certainly broke out of that. So, the one on politics of British society in the 1930s, oh,

I just remember enjoying that so much. I remember, we had to volunteer to do a paper. [The course] was taught as a seminar, which was also incredibly exciting and unusual. And I researched the Left Book Club, which was great, and actually there's a link there to Mass Observation, because as far as I remember, Tom Harrisson came to that, and probably told me I had got it all wrong. But he was around, and he did occasionally appear at different things. So I think he listened to me talking about the Left Book Club, and then, you know, I think, I can't remember what he said, but basically he then did his presentation on the Left Book Club. [Laughing]

To rectify the lack of women's or gender history in the university courses, Summerfield and others created their own opportunities.

PS: There were lots of extracurricular activities at Sussex, and one of the things that, certainly from my second year, from 1971 to 1972, that I got really swept up into was the Women's Liberation Movement. And WLM had loads of little groups – it's famous for this – it had consciousness raising groups, and health groups, and motor mechanics groups, and a women's history group. So, I really enjoyed becoming a member of the women's history group, and we made up for the shortcomings of the curriculum, without actually being terribly, explicitly critical of the curriculum. But we decided we were going to study women revolutionaries and reformers, so we studied Clara Zetkin, Emma Goldman, Alexandra Kolontai and Sylvia Pankhurst and the other Pankhursts. See, we didn't like the other Pankhursts because they were too right wing. We liked Sylvia! [laughing].

Summerfield initially decided to explain the result of the 1945 election by researching Army Education and the Army Bureau of Current Affairs. This led her to the Mass-Observation Archive for the first time. Summerfield's advisor, Stephen Yeo, encouraged her to consult the materials.

PS: So off I went, up, to the top floor of this building. Lovely and light. And there all these black stacks, with lots of big thick cardboard boxes on them, and round the corner of one of the stacks, came Dorothy, who was then Dorothy Wainwright, to become Dorothy Sheridan. And, I explained what I was after, and she was very helpful and found a box in which was a complete jumble of material. And she said none of this is catalogued or listed, but we did a deal. She said I could use it if I would list it as I went through it. So, I did that. It wasn't a proper cataloguing job, because I didn't have those skills. But, I did make her a list, and I sort of organized it in columns: the date, the name, the subject, a little tiny summary of what was there. And I did find stuff. I mean, in terms of my project at that time, it wasn't sort of spot on. I was researching the policy in the War Office towards Army Education. I wanted to know why Churchill had complained about it, who backed it, what they wanted from it. But I was really keen to find out more about the receiving end, and how men in the forces responded to the education, to the compulsory current affairs classes they had to do one hour a week, they were supposed to do. The War Office produced these pamphlets, which they wrote on topics, like, oh I don't know – the Suez Canal, or Russia in the War, or I think there was even one on something like Women and Welfare. There was certainly one of the Beveridge Report – that was highly controversial, and Churchill insisted on it being withdrawn. Anyway, so I was fascinated, but I really wanted to know from below – from below – what the reception was like. And what I found in these Mass-Observation boxes were two things: (1) that it wasn't like other Mass-Observation material in that, if you were called up into the military, you weren't allowed to keep a diary, so there weren't any diaries for security reasons and you weren't allowed to write reports on what was going on. However, there were no – there was censorship of letters – but you could write letters. So, most of that material was individuals' letters to Tom Harrisson usually, or Bob Willcock, sort of 'Here I am stuck in Cumberland at an Army Training camp. Everybody is browned off. I feel like I'm wasting my time'. It was that sort of thing. It certainly gave me a sense of the context. And there were just a few, little bits about Army Education in it. I was looking in the publication that arose from that research and I was surprised to see that I'd footnoted there was sixteen such letters, so sixteen people, men I'm afraid – this is another issue, mind – had kept going in terms of their contact with MO, and wrote about what it was like to be called up into one or another of the armed forces. So I certainly got a lot of the context of what it was like to go from being a civilian to being part of the armed forces, and their observations of the other recruits around them, the sort of training they had, their feelings about the high-ups, and there was lots of disrespect for the officer class. [Laughs] It was great stuff. I think what it gave me for that project was a sort of capacity to talk about what the army high-ups were addressing. They were worried that the civilian conscripts were discontented, not motivated, ill-informed, and that's why they wanted to have army education. And, certainly the Mass-Observation material supported that idea.

While Summerfield found the M-O material intriguing, it also threw up some challenges.

PS: There were no guides on how to do this. I was just aware that I wanted history from below, as well as from above, and that it was important to tap into that. It was quite scary in a way, because I was quite new to doing research, and it's all very well going to the Public Record Office, where the files are all orderly and you can see the logic of it, you can see the civil servant's hand filing them all neatly. And you often get summaries of the things that have been discussed and it's all there – there's a story there.

[M-O] was more difficult to use, but utterly fascinating. Utterly fascinating. I think that some of the people who were writing were actually quite well known. And one was named John Somerfield – nothing to do, different spelling from my own name, but obviously, the name stuck in my mind. He was a novelist, and I'd come across him in that course on the 1930s that I'd done, but I was fascinated to find his letters there. He was saying things like, 'I should've stayed a civilian, with Mass-Observation, I'd be doing more good for the war effort – as a Mass Observer, than I am stuck up here in this Army camp doing absolutely nothing.' Only he used ruder language!

Experience with the Mass-Observation archive compelled Summerfield to seek out more direct responses from veterans.

PS: The Mass Observation stuff was so tantalizing and so interesting that I thought maybe there are other ways of getting at this from below. And, I did my first independent oral history project, interviewing fourteen men, who I found through pieces in local newspapers, I think in three different towns. They responded about army education, so they could tell me more about the actual experience of army education.

The research on Army Education and the Army Bureau of Current Affairs would later be published in the International Review of Social History,[8] *but Summerfield decided to change the focus of her doctoral thesis research. Summerfield remembers the research seminar that influenced this decision:*

PS: There I was working away on army education – politics and education in the armed forces – and I gave a seminar as research students were expected to do, in probably 1975–6. And one of the other postgrads said to me, as a question, in the seminar – '[the paper] had been really interesting, but Penny, what about women in the armed forces? Did they get army education and current affairs discussions?' And I was stumped. There I was, a feminist, a member of the Women's Liberation Movement, who'd been in this Women's History group that we'd been reading and researching all these women in history, and it hadn't actually *occurred* to me that I ought to study the history of women. That's not entirely true. I'd thought of it in terms of the course I did on revolutions. And, you know, I'd been told, 'oh no, no, no, you can't do women in revolutions. There isn't enough material.' And I'd done my dissertation for that course on peasants. Not that peasants aren't women, *sometimes*! But that was the attitude. Don't do women, there's not enough there – you can't do that. And as far as the army education work was concerned, I certainly hadn't come across anything about women in all the papers I'd been reading – both in the official archives and in Mass-Observation. I really hadn't. So when Debbie, this friend, this fellow postgrad in the seminar, said, 'what about women?',

I was kind of gobsmacked. It was a real moment of illumination. I thought how could I possibly carry on doing all this stuff about blokes? You know? I'm a feminist, I ought to be doing women's history. And women's history wasn't a thing. This is 1975–6. It was barely was a thing. I mean, it probably was more in the States, but Sussex University didn't have women's history.

Summerfield's doctoral research shifted focus to women workers during the Second World War, which was eventually published as Women Workers in the Second World War: Production and Patriarchy in Conflict.⁹ *Summerfield concurrently collaborated with fellow Sussex postgrad, Gail Braybon, to publish* Out of the Cage: Women's Experiences in Two World Wars.¹⁰

PS: One of my great friends became Gail Braybon. And Gail and I embarked on postgrad work, I think a year apart, but I can't remember in which direction. I started on my DPhil, and she'd opted to do an MPhil. I can't really remember why, because you know, it seems daft now, you'd see I would advise any student who had ambitions to set their sights on a DPhil rather than an MPhil. But anyway, she did her MPhil on women workers in the First World War, and that had a great impact on me. I had not been working for my DPhil on women, but partly under the influence of Gail, I switched and decided it was all going to be on women. And, Stephen [Yeo], my supervisor, was a bit doubtful about this sudden switch because I was more than a year, probably two years into it. I said, 'no, that's what I'm going to do, that's what I'm going to do.' And so, Gail and I decided 'right, well, we'll each publish our own book': hers on women workers in the First World War and mine on women workers in the Second World War, but we always had in mind it would be nice to collaborate, and once we'd got those done and published, we did collaborate and we wrote *Out of the Cage: Women's Experiences in Two World Wars* together.

For my thesis and my first book – *Women Workers in the Second World War* – I certainly used official policy and I found it absolutely fascinating, because I found this tussle between the need for women's labour in the labour force and the pull from other parts of the same government, the same state, that called to keep women in the home, and that wonderful, interesting conflict really, so fascinating, and that was in the official archives. Mass-Observation was absolutely wonderful for enabling me to tap into how women felt about things like being mobilized, you know the various steps towards conscription and direction of women, and eventually in Dec 1941 the conscription of certain age groups, certain marital statuses of women. How did they feel about it? I think the amazing, amazing thing about Mass-Observation is that it *shocks*. It wasn't a kind of 'oh, yes, we're willing, we're willing, we'll rush into the factories, we want to do war work!' It was a load of women saying 'oh no, that looks really boring', when they were at War Work Week exhibitions, or kind of chatting to each other overheard conversations, 'oh my husband wouldn't half kick up if I went off to a factory, I don't think I could do that.' And then, Celia Fremlin's study in the war factory. Huge amounts of alienation from the labour process from the kind of work they were expected to do. Mass-Observation gave you very different sort of picture.

One of the amazing things about MO when I was using it, in the 1970s and 1980s, was Dorothy [Sheridan], particularly, but the other people working, kept finding new things, because it was unplumbed. And they were gradually working through sorting it all out, cataloguing it, and one of the things that came to light were the letters of the women welders. So, these were women who were trained by a Mass-Observer, and when they'd finished their training, and they went off to factories – they were in Huddersfield and Penistone in Yorkshire – and they corresponded with their trainer, and she didn't ask them, because you didn't in those days, she gave all their letters to Mass-Observation. And, you know, that's a treasure, that's amazing! I remember using those in *Out of the Cage*. And then, Margaretta Jolly published a very nice book, an anthology of the letters, with good commentary that she wrote herself.

Summerfield views both oral history and the materials collected by Mass-Observation as important ways of accessing experience. She reflects on both the difference and complementarity of these sources:

PS: I see them as two different sorts of ways of tapping into experience, of subjectivity and narrative and the way people talk about the past. They are very different methodologically, because you're doing such different things. If you're working through a box full of different types of documents, which is what the Mass-Observation archive is like, [there are] so many different types of documents. I started with letters, but there are the directive replies, the diaries, there are the observations in the street, there are the reports, the file reports, there are things like wonderful Celia Fremlin's study of the War Factory, which is just so brilliant; she was sent incognito into Michael Lipman's radar factory called Ekco in Gloucestershire and wrote her report, [which] was published as *War Factory*. So there are the publications, as well as all the other materials, which should not be underrated. And of course, *now*, post-81, there are all the post-81 directive replies, which is another thing again. There's no simple way of comparing that abundance of very, very textual material with oral history. Both types of material give access to experience, everyday life, and certainly the way I think about it now, the way people construct their stories about themselves: their histories of the self. I certainly saw them as complementary.

That early experience of Mass Observation really made me feel that the everyday and the – I know ordinary person is quite a loaded phrase – but still the ordinary person were just terribly important in history. And I didn't want to find myself writing history that didn't tap into their experience, the experience of the everyday, the experience of being *not* one of the elite, not a leader, but an ordinary person. So, certainly, Mass Observation showed me, from an early stage, this is possible. You can do this. And oral history helped that on its way. So, that's been terribly important in all of the work I've done. I also got interested in Mass Observation as an organization. You know, I started, there's two parts to this: one in the 1980s and one in the 1990s. In the 1980s, I remember I was at Lancaster and somebody asked me if I would do a research seminar on Mass Observation. Not asking me to do something on army education or women in the war. They were asking me to talk about Mass Observation, and that made me fascinated to think about it as an organization. And out of that came an article I published, I think in about 1985, 'Mass-Observation: Social Research or Social Movement?'[11] And I felt, in many ways, it was both. It had a campaigning dimension to it, and that I found very interesting.

Summerfield reflects on shifts in historiographical thinking and the ways in which the Mass-Observation Archive and researchers were part of those new ways of thinking:

In the 1990s, I mean we'd all, sort of, if we hadn't taken the cultural turn, we'd become aware of the ideas of discourse, and of post-structural ideas, perhaps that loosened up thinking in many ways? I started to think about, particularly the Mass-Observation publications as contributing to public discourse: as part of conversations about women, about war, about what the war effort was, about how it should be conducted, but at a level of the text. Rather than thinking of Mass Observation always as a window onto the past and experience and so on. So, that, in addition to, seeing it as a way of tapping into individual experience.

One of the big things, one of the liberations that the cultural turn enabled was to give historians confidence about not being quantitative. Mass Observation itself was hung up on 'are we quantitative or are we qualitative?' And at the time, you could hardly not try to claim a sort of quantitative or statistical respectability. Tom Harrisson certainly tried desperately with all his weird statistics, you know where you had percentages, and you didn't know what the total number was and you'd have no sense of the reliability of the statistics. At the same time [M-O was] collecting masses and masses of clearly absolutely wonderful and invaluable material, full of insights which couldn't be quantified, just couldn't be quantified. Like the diaries: how could you quantify them? And the observations, because they didn't use standard questionnaires. It was very different from the wartime social survey, for example, under his friend Mary Adams, which did. But you know, sometimes, like with the opinion polls, sometimes, the answers that he – or Mass-Observation – got out of their materials in a non-statistical way were completely consistent with what was coming through quantitative methods. So that was that then. Talking about historians particularly I think in the 1990s and the 2000s, I think working with Mass-Observation in the context of the cultural turn gave historians the confidence to say, 'I am not making statistical generalizations. I am using material which is extraordinarily special in enabling us to understand people's subjective responses, and it's special not because these people were exceptional, but because they were ordinary.' However, they wrote down their ordinary everyday lives and their ordinary, everyday thoughts, and their observations of each other and of what was going on. And they're different from the rest of the population that, as far as we know, and on the whole, didn't write it down. Michael Rustin, a sociologist, used a wonderful phrase, 'The luminosity of the individual case.' And I often think of that now, when I'm using Mass-Observation material. It has this luminosity, it has this way of literally casting light, on what we want to know about, or what we realize now we want to know about [laughing]. When I'm talking about this, I'm thinking of a number of key historians. Lucy Noakes in her book *War and the British* uses Mass Observation in that way, with a confidence, that these people they're ordinary, everyday people. We can, as it were, rely on them to give us a take on what was happening that may not be representative of what loads and loads of people were thinking, but was one way in which people were reacting to the Falklands War or to the Gulf War, and it's valuable, all the more valuable because of their ability to write it down. James Hinton would be another one. *9 Wartime Lives* I think is one of my favourite books, I absolutely love it. Again, he justifies what he's doing on the grounds that these people were in a special position to observe themselves and to observe those around them and to record their observations, because they're writing for Mass Observation. Tony Kushner shouldn't be forgotten, either, with his book on anti-Semitism which uses Mass Observation – very much the same spirit... Claire Langhamer later, a bit later, more like the 2000s and her book *The English in Love,* uses directive replies, again in very much the same spirit. So, you know, in a *sense, Mass Observation has made us understand the value of qualitative material for accessing everyday life for ordinary people.*

The qualitative diversity of responses within the Mass-Observation materials can challenge researchers and students who are concerned about the representativeness of the Observers and their writing.

PS: I certainly notice among students, because of the way they've been educated in school history, they worry, 'Is it biased?' Oh, the length of time I've tried to explain to students that bias is not a helpful concept when dealing with something like Mass Observation. And also, 'can I generalize?', and 'will what I do be valid if I can't generalize?' Well, everybody's different, you're different, I'm different, you know, no two people are just the same. And the great value of Mass Observation is to tap into this enormous diversity, this enormous variety. At the same time, you know, especially something like the diaries, gives a lot to go on – a lot of context. You can situate people, where they belong socially within society, and politically, and ethnically, and regionally, and in terms of age, and Mass Observation is so sensitive to all those things. And, you know, you're able, one is able to say more because one has this wider context. So it's writing up not just about the individual, but about the world they live in.

Summerfield reflects on the current challenges to the post-1981 Mass Observation Project, as well as its richness of responses and immense opportunity.

PS: What would be desirable, especially now: greater diversity. I know that Dorothy worried about this, and I'm sure that the current people in charge of the post-81 project are concerned about it. It's very tricky. You know you want perhaps fewer white women in their sixties from the southeast of England – white middle-class women in their sixties – and you want more young working-class men, and you definitely want more Black people, and Asians, and maybe people with disabilities, and from Northern Ireland, as well as the whole of the rest of Britain. It's very hard to do, and I'm not quite sure how it can be achieved, but it's sort of worth wrestling with that problem. Because it's a writing project, and a lot of people like writing. It's sort of a technological thing – but I [also] think it's very important – it would be so much easier if they all emailed in their answers, instead of printing them out and posting them. It seems to me a very easy step towards cheap and immediate digitization. You just say to people – everybody can use a computer now, if there are a few people who can't, that's fine – but the norm needs to be use a computer and send it in online. Then it's digitized, and it's so much more accessible to researchers.

Each time I've engaged with Mass Observation for a different project, over time, something completely unexpected has come out of it. I did commission a directive a few years ago – I think about 2009 – about memory of the [Second World] War and how it had featured in people's childhood, schooling and adult life. My directive was basically, 'how has the memory of World War Two impacted on your life?' And then there were prompts like, 'what kind of impression of World War Two did you get from your schooling?' or later, 'did you enjoy – not enjoy would be too loaded – did you go to the cinema and see wartime films?' and 'have family memories been passed down in your family?', that kind of thing. I found the replies absolutely wonderful, really fascinating. And what I've discovered, which I'd never expected to discover, was that people who replied, who were really across the age spectrum, whatever age they were, they seemed to be talking about generations. 'The previous generation found World War Two really important', or 'my generation really understands what World War Two was all about', or 'my generation can only respect the stories of our elders', or 'my generation finds World War Two completely strange and foreign and alienating.' And I thought, 'wow! They're all using the concept of World War Two as a way of building their own generational identity.' Would I have thought of that before I did the project? No. So, I suppose what I'm saying about that is just the potentiality for creative thinking, new kinds of approaches to history, is just *there* in that amazing, amazing wealth of material.

Dorothy Sheridan

Professor Dorothy Sheridan, MBE, began working with Tom Harrisson and the Mass-Observation archive at Sussex University in the mid-1970s. From 1990 to 2010, she served as Director of the Mass Observation Archive at the University and served as a Trustee of the Archive from 2010 to 2020. Sheridan was born in Galway, Ireland. When she was very young, her parents moved to London and then to Yorkshire.

DS: [My parents] remained determinedly Irish, but not in an Irish community, which I think was quite hard. But they defined themselves as 'bohemian'. They were Irish Republicans and my father sang and played lots of musical instruments and my mother read a lot. They really attracted a random – a kind of coterie of what you might call intellectual lefties, folk singers, at a time when folk singing was part of the general radical movement. With the early campaign for nuclear disarmament and anti-Vietnam war. Eventually, they became very much more involved in politics and in alternative politics, and in poetry and theatre and stuff like that whenever they could. And they were always having parties and drinking lots of whiskey. It was a bit chaotic. But I went to this very respectable grammar school and kept my two worlds quite apart. I was proud of my parents. I believed in what they believed in; I never really rebelled against them. I went on to be a socialist and a feminist, like my mother. I went on the early Aldermaston marches with my parents. So, from the age of twelve, I was involved in oppositional campaigning and stuff like that.

Sheridan's upbringing drew her to Sussex, which had a reputation for non-traditional teaching and radical politics.

DS: Sussex had a reputation at that time for being a radical university. Asa Briggs, he wasn't the Vice Chancellor then, but he was Professor of History then, and there were a number of [other] people at Sussex. So, when I heard about it, even though it seemed like a different country from Yorkshire, my teachers didn't approve, but I was really keen. So keen, in fact, that when I failed to get into Sussex the first time (they interviewed me and gave me a place, but my A-levels weren't good enough), I took my A-levels again to get the As I needed. It was quite competitive to get into Sussex, and I got in the second time. So I had a special kind of gratitude to Sussex because they gave me a second chance.

After being admitted to Sussex, Sheridan studied Sociology. She explains:

DS: Sociology was the interesting subject. I think I've learned since then that lots of young women wanted to go to places like Sussex and Essex and study Sociology, ahem, I thought I was being so original, but really

I was part of the *zeitgeist*. Sussex had, at that time, an interdisciplinary structure which allowed you to choose where you studied sociology. There were schools of study: a School of English and American studies, and a School of Educational studies, which is what I did, and a School of African and Asian studies. And you could study a major in any of those. It was one of the things that went after a while. But at the beginning, that was what marked Sussex out. There were a number of people at Sussex that I'd heard of in that, in Sociology as well, and Sussex was also hosting quite a lot of radical philosophers and thinkers from Eastern Europe. I was able to pick and choose courses in a way that you probably couldn't now. But I did Marxism one term, and reproductive rights in another term, and you know, it was like doing evening classes really. I didn't have to think, at that time, about my career, or what it was all preparing me for. I just thought, 'oooh, what would I like to do next term?' It was a different time.

Sheridan met and married her first husband, Tony, while at Sussex. She later met her second husband, Barry, who became their lodger while he studied for his PGCE. Sheridan began work with Tom Harrisson in 1974.

DS: I always remember, we were living in Lewes at that time. Tom Harrisson, who I think was a bit intrigued by me, said he was going to come and visit me, which terrified me – I was absolutely terrified by Tom Harrisson. And he came an hour early. And of course, found me and Tony and Barry completely unready. But mostly what I was worried about was that I hadn't any real coffee, I only had instant coffee to give him. I felt ashamed! [laughing] But I'm sure he did that deliberately. It was a very typical Tom Harrisson thing, to try and catch me, uh, to learn more about me and to get me on the hop, you know?

I met Barry in 1974, and I started work at Mass-Observation in 1974. So, unfortunately for historians, I say more in my diary about Barry than I do about Tom Harrisson! Which really annoys me now. [laughing] It was the same summer. I took this very part-time job in the library at Sussex. Because in fact, I'd been away from Sussex. Tony and I lived in Scotland for a while, but I'd come back because Tony got a job at Sussex. I just started in a job that made portable traffic lights and signals, and I had just learned about all the electronic parts for it when a friend in a woman's group I was in said, 'Oh, I work for this eccentric old professor. Would you like to take over my job? I want to go and do teacher training.' And I said, 'Oh no, I've just started at the traffic light factory.' You know, [her friend said], 'For goodness sake, Dorothy, this is at the University and you'll get two telephones.' [Laughing] I remember, she said, 'What do you know, can you type?' I said, 'No, I can't type.' She said 'It's about the Second World War,' meaning the archive. Of course, I had no family memory, no history of the Second World War, because we'd come to England after the war. But I said I'd have a go, it was more or less to do her a favour, really. And that's when I first met Tom Harrisson. It was August 1974, and he was just about to do a BBC program on wartime propaganda film, and the camera and the film crew were due the next day, after my interview with him. So, my interview with him consisted of me having to write labels to stick up on the shelves: a thing I have done many times since. Nothing to do with what's in the boxes, but of course the boxes, at that time, were in the room I was in. They were all around me, so I had to stick up labels that looked interesting, like money, sex, war. [Laughing]

Sheridan remembers working with Harrisson:

DS: He wasn't there [at Sussex] very often. He lived in Brussels at this time. He came over once a term, although that one day a term was the most petrifying. Most of the time, he wasn't there. But he also issued commands for me. That was when I first started to learn about the collection, but not in a way maybe that was a good way, because he would say – he was working on *Living through the Blitz* at that time and he needed accounts of people being bombed. So he'd say, 'Can you get me something about somebody being bombed in Liverpool?' Well, I just looked at all these boxes, and, you know, I didn't even know when the Liverpool blitz was. It was a fast-learning curve, but I was motivated. I managed to send him enough material to keep him happy, I think. So, really, I was more a kind of research assistant. Nobody else used the collection until a year later or so. So I wasn't running a service. Gradually people started to want to have access, and Tom gave me very strict instructions about people: who could come in, who could come in before lunch, but not after lunch, because he had a thing about people with drink problems, he said. He was completely paranoid and very possessive. I think I inherited a bit of that from him, or it rubbed off on me a bit.

[Harrisson] put me in a small office with all the Worktown books, all the Worktown boxes, all the File Reports. They were all in these wartime cabinets with no anti-tilt mechanism, and they used to fall on me all the time, because every time I opened a drawer it would come towards me. [laughing] He wanted to do a book on Worktown. He also thought that the File Reports were perhaps the most valuable because they were the summaries of everything. He'd also planned a book on royalty. And he was planning his autobiography. So, he didn't want anybody else to get in there, but then he was killed very suddenly in a bus accident in Thailand in January 1976. So, that was the end of my time working with him.

As Vice-Chancellor of Sussex, Asa Briggs was instrumental in bringing several important collections to Sussex, including the Mass-Observation Archive, the Virginia and Leonard Woolf Monk's House Papers and Rudyard Kipling's Papers.

DS: Angus [Calder] had used Mass-Observation material when it was still in London for *The People's War*. And Paul Addison, who is a Professor of History at Edinburgh; then he was a postgraduate – he did a book called *The Road to 45*, and he used Mass Observation. And Angus wrote to Asa Briggs, [who] was Angus's supervisor. I found a letter that Angus wrote to Asa saying, 'Look, there's this collection in London that I think it should either come to Sussex, or the Nuffield College.' I don't know why Nuffield. 'But, it's a wonderful collection and it should be somewhere and being looked after.' So that was in a way what brought it to Asa's attention. Asa then liaised with the current director of Mass-Observation, who was a man called Len England, a very nice man, that I did meet, who arranged to have it transported to Sussex. But not before quite a lot of material – not the handwritten or typed stuff – but much of the ephemera was sent to the Imperial War Museum. It's interesting to me that that was what was regarded as the most valuable – the labels and the posters. A lot did come to Sussex, but a lot of it went to the Imperial War Museum and joined their print/ephemera collection, like that was the most important bit of it, which of course to me isn't, but anyway. So, it was Asa Briggs liaising with Len England of Mass-Observation UK Limited, who arranged for the material to come to Sussex. And when it came to Sussex, it was actually stored in the Vice-Chancellor's office. They had bigger offices then, I think, and only gradually did it get put into the library.

Asa invited Tom [Harrisson] to Sussex, and Tom managed to get a grant from the Leverhulme Trust to put it in boxes. So by the time I worked for him, he'd got archival quality boxes and he'd used a number of temporary staff – temporary, but very dedicated, staff – to get it into the boxes, not all of it, but most of it. Which didn't mean it was sorted, it was just in the boxes. And that was probably 1970, 1971, I think, and between then and seventy-four when I came along, Harrisson was tasked by Asa Briggs to promote the archive, so the aim was, to make it a public research resource in the University. Because Asa, at that time, had also invited a number of other archival collections, in fact some of the really important collections at Sussex were from Asa's time, you know, like the Virginia and Leonard Woolf Monks House papers, Rudyard Kipling's archive – that was a deal done with the National Trust – were all brought in by Asa Briggs at that time. And that's why I think Sussex's special collections were actually – for a new university – quite a good, important resource. I think that Asa was looking around to bring things to Sussex that would make it unique, and Mass-Observation was one of them.

With Mass-Observation materials installed at Sussex in the mid-1970s, but not yet fully catalogued, the question of when to open the archive to researchers was paramount. Since Sheridan did not have experience or training as an archivist, she found she had to learn on the job.

DS: I think there was always a tension – there always is with archives I think – how much do you catalogue it first, and then make it available, for security reasons and just to know what you've got. It was very difficult; there's always been that tension, but then no resources to catalogue it. Leverhulme had given money for boxes and we gradually got bits of money to do other things, but it was slow work, and if you don't let researchers have access, you lose potential informed support. I mean I've always found that the biggest allies I had in promoting the archive were the people who used it, you know the people who knew its value, like Angus Calder, like Penny [Summerfield], like Nick Stanley. Those people got to know it very well, and were very useful to me: it was in discussions with people like them that I learned about the archive. I learned more about how it could be used. I spent a lot of time with those people, I think, at the beginning. And, for a long time, if people didn't talk to me they wouldn't know how to find things, because there were only a few limited finding aids. And even [though] my knowledge wasn't that great, I was one step ahead of people. But I sometimes, over the years, would be looking at what somebody was working at and I thought, 'Ooh, they could look at this as well'. That's why now, with it all being digitized, it's just incredible that you can search, even handwriting now. And it did depend so much on [my] memory in those days.

But then, I didn't have a qualification as an archivist, I was a sociology graduate. I did look into getting a qualification, but Sussex wouldn't have seconded me and the only courses were really rather old-fashioned courses in London. I would have had to commute and what with a little boy to look after, I didn't feel I could. It would have meant learning paleography, it wouldn't have been relevant to a twentieth-century collection. So, I stayed, and I decided to put myself on a self-education program. I went round visiting other archives – other modern archives, like the Modern Records Centre at Warwick, which has Trade Union and radical group records. I had a lot of support from the archivist at the Royal Observatory, you know the Astronomer Royal's archivist, because the Royal Observatory was at Herstmonceux, which was in Sussex. And, although I assumed at first that it was all about stars, they actually have lots of material about the area where they're situated, going back many years, and because it originally had been at Greenwich, there was loads of material about Greenwich. So, I had some very nice friends who were archivists who took me under their wing. Luckily, luckily, I don't think I did any damage. I didn't go around putting Sellotape on anything or moving things around too much – that was the other problem. Using or imagining that a library type cataloguing system would work with archives is misguided, since the fundamental principle of archives management, or arrangement, is the principle of provenance. You try to keep things as they were generated to reflect the history of the enterprise. Not easy with a collection like Mass-Observation, because it was a working collection; until really 1970, nobody thought of it as an archive. Over the years, the Mass-Observers thought of it as their own working papers to be used and re-used. So, I'd be looking through something about gambling in 1949 and find suddenly, an observation from Bolton, 1939. And go, 'Oh! What's this doing here? It's from an entirely different study!' But that's because they were put in together, and the people working on it had no concept of provenance. Why should they? I always remember, a former Mass-Observer, one of the people who was brought in as a field worker in wartime who came down to Sussex to visit. She went through the papers of projects she'd been involved in producing and working on, and got out her red biro and started writing all over it! [As the Observer:] 'Oh, this shouldn't be here and we never finished this, and I'll just do this!' And I stood there watching her, completely paralysed, because I thought, 'You can't write on archives with red biro!' On the other hand, she had generated it in the first place. You know?

I think that the popular image of an archivist when I first started was of some very scholarly erudite academic person, not an informational professional – rather, somebody who was an expert in the field and history of the archive, and not necessarily a teacher, or a person wanting to share. There used to be a lot of criticism of archivists for being obstructive gatekeepers. A bit like Umberto Eco's novel, *The Name of the Rose*, you know the very grave librarian in that; that was the image, almost monastic. And yet, I knew that to survive, and it was not just the archive's survival, but my own, keeping my job – I started to be in love with my job. The survival of the archive and of my career were intertwined, that if I was going to survive, I was going to have to get money, and get friends, and show that Mass-Observation could be useful to research and teaching. Because there were a number of people, and Tom Harrisson knew this too, who rubbished Mass-Observation completely.

Sheridan reflects on the criticisms aimed at Mass-Observation and its methods, as well as notions of representativeness:

DS: There was a kind of feeling that the only people who would keep diaries – and some of this is true, but it needs taking apart – were people with the leisure, the material resources and the literacy skills to be able to write as they did. So it wasn't working-class history, and therefore for many social historians of the time, it wasn't valuable. Asa Briggs (as Vice Chancellor) organized a launch party in 1975, inviting the people that were most interested in Mass-Observation: anthropologists and some social historians, feminist historians, Literary and art historians, but not traditional social historians, not really, and not sociologists, who saw it as being amateurish, biased, dubious, not scientific, who were rooted in a much more positivist approach. That gave all of us a bit of a challenge. I think people like Penny and Nick, and others, and Angus, were criticized for relying on something so subjective. And so, what I started to want to show was that the subjectivity of Mass-Observation was an asset, it was a resource, that people telling their own stories was a resource. And that you couldn't understand Mass-Observation without understanding issues about literacy, language behaviour or the cultural position of writing which was both gendered and class-based. Trying to show that, as long as you understood what the influences were, as long as you took them into account, Mass-Observation texts could be a very valuable resource, particularly, for example, if you wanted to understand women's history. And I stopped thinking of the people who were part of the panel as data subjects (I'm not sure that was what I was taught when I did my Sociology degree, but there was a bit of that). Better to think of the writers as more like reporters, or citizen journalists, or windows on a world. So, methodologically, there was a big argument to be won. I have stood up at so many conferences over the years, in so many places, to talk to people about the question of statistical representativeness. One of the problems is it that the Mass-Observation 'panel' was deceptively large – so many people took part, so many people answered directives, so many people kept diaries – that it looks like a social sample, a small social sample admittedly. Whereas, if you were doing an oral history – and some of these same critics were doing oral histories with, say, only twelve people, the sample size could be valid. And, what I'm trying to say is that it was a bit like a big oral history project, written not oral. You learn things from this kind of material that you don't learn in other ways.

You could say that oral historians were my best mates at the time. They were the people who were tackling some of the same issues. Not long before he died, Tom Harrisson and Paul Thompson, the oral historian from Essex, clashed a little bit, because Harrisson argued against memory; he said memory was fallible. And Paul Thompson critiqued Mass-Observation as unreliable, and somewhere there's a review of Harrisson's *Living through the Blitz*, by Paul Thompson where he more or less says this. [Thompson] felt very hurt because there's a whole chapter in *Living through the Blitz* about memory and about the things people don't remember or do remember, and how faulty it is. Harrisson in turn accepted some of the things that people said about oral history not being reliable. And that meant that Paul Thompson responded quite vigorously in return. I felt a bit caught between them, because I knew both of them and respected them both in different ways.

In the mid-1980s when I was doing my own research, I joined a little discussion group with the Australian oral historian, Al Thomson and Graham Dawson of the Popular Memory Group at Birmingham (both Al and Graham were at that time writing their doctoral theses). One of the things that we talked about was the impact of popular memory on recall, the ways in which memory operates, what people are able to say, the silences in oral testimony, the language that is available to people at different stages of their lives, the impact of cultural transformations, and on how, over time, different stories can be told. [These concerns] work with Mass-Observation just as much as with oral history. I think that Al was one of the first people to start looking at this, and Penny [Summerfield] picked up on it, and started using his idea of composing memory. Al was very much influenced by Graham, who isn't an oral historian, but was concerned with the impact of cultural understandings. Inevitably, both Al and Graham had a big influence on me.

Al and I then – we'd been teaching together in adult education for a while – decided to set up a Masters Degree in Life History Research. He did the oral history aspects; I did the life writing part. He covered technical things about the practice of interviewing people; I covered approaches to using written archives. But then we came together and the students each did a project. They could either choose an oral history project or an archival project, but we did one combined course on methodology and interpretation – a whole term – on how people tell their stories. This was relevant to both oral testimony and written testimony in different ways. Al has done a lot of work since then on comparing people's stories at different stages of their lives or on comparing the formats – media – letters, photographs, diaries, interviews, and how different things work out. I think I benefitted enormously from having the space to explore those things with Al and our students. That course lasted about five or six years.

Al went back to Australia in 2007 and by then, I had been promoted within the University Library. My career was taking off in different directions really. In the end, I couldn't do what amounted to five jobs (teaching and research, senior Library admin including management of all the Special Collections, and archiving!). There was always a tension, even right through all the years when I was trying to promote and raise money for the archive, because I also was obliged to play a key role in the University Library. For example, for several years, I selected and catalogued all the history books in the Library, which was quite fun, but took up a lot of time away from Mass-Observation. It had a plus side – kept me quite rooted in another world.

Sussex Professor of Sociology, David Pocock, took over the Mass-Observation archive after Tom Harrisson's death. Several years later, in 1981, he and Sheridan initiated the Mass Observation Project.

DS: [David Pocock] was a senior person in the University, and I think he was given the archive just to keep an eye on it. But his academic career was going off in different directions, and he decided in 1981 that he wanted to spend more time in the archive, and so he decided to see if we could recruit new writers. There had been an attempt in 1977, with the historian and author, Philip Ziegler. For the Queen's Silver Jubilee, Philip Ziegler set up a little panel. It seemed to be mostly made up of his friends and acquaintances. David got interested in that and, as part of the Silver Jubilee Project, put out a call for descriptions of street parties. Many people sent in street party observations. These were not published at the time. Then, in 1981, the year of the Royal Wedding, David decided to see if we could get people to respond to Mass-Observation style 'directives'. We had no extra money to finance this idea except for a little bit of money from the Leverhulme Trust which was originally meant to be a year of my salary. But now my salary was being paid for by the University, so David said let's use it to recruit new volunteers. So, that's what we did, through the national and local newspapers and local radio. And at first, I have to tell you, I was not happy. Our small office didn't have any storage space, and we had no extra money and I had no extra staffing help, and yet we were just beginning to be used by visiting researchers who placed a welcome but substantial demand on us. We started having this huge amount of material coming in by post every day. But I admit that eventually the project seduced me; I think the aspect of Mass-Observation that I liked was this participatory sense. I believed, or accepted, the idea of a democratic form of social science – not that I think you can ever get rid of the power relations between an academic institution and the people who contribute, but, I did think it would be good for people to write about their lives in their own voices.

David Pocock was not interested in going on the front line to defend what he was doing methodologically. So I had to do it, really; I had to say why it was worth doing. Also, I felt so privileged to have so much of what people were offering, and I liked the interaction with people, because they would suggest ideas, or criticize; some of them were very critical. Anyway, they hero-worshipped David, because they thought he was this perfect, elderly professor that they were writing to, which was a problem when he left, because people were bereft. But, they still wrote, and I've always believed that people write – once they got going – they write for themselves, partly for themselves, and it didn't really matter whether it was me or David at the other end. Sometimes they'd talk about 'the ladies of the archive' (that is me and my tiny team of part-time helpers). And so, by the end of the 1990s, we had over 1,000 people writing for us. That had to be managed at the same time as we were offering a research service. We tried to offer four days a week to be open. It was good because it meant that we weren't 'a dead archive'.

Observers from both the mid-century Mass-Observation and the post-1981 Mass Observation Project often expected that their writing would be read by Mass-Observation staff or 'the ladies of the archive'. Sheridan discusses observers' varied motivations for writing and interactions with the Mass Observation Project:

DS: I was always struck by one of the writers from the war period, who, I don't know whether she said in so many words, but it was quite clear that she felt isolated. She came from somewhere in the north, northeast, Gateshead. She had a daughter who suffered from epilepsy and it was a struggle for her. It was obvious, she was very lonely, unhappy. She once said was how helpful it was for her to write to the people in London, like Tom Harrisson, who were educated and sympathetic and knowledgeable and humane. I thought that over-rated Tom Harrisson, frankly, but I could see why she felt that the people in London were going to be more accepting of her with her problems. It was important for [Observers] to be valued, and to feel that what they were doing was of value. I've seen letters where people have said, 'I'm not writing anymore because I can see that you're not reading what I've written.' So it wasn't that it didn't matter [who read what they sent] but it didn't matter precisely who it was, because they would create their own image of who it was that was important for their fantasy about writing and it encouraged them. When we started sending out the directives again, they were written like letters; it amounted to a correspondence, a dialogue, which sometimes needs to be replenished. People did say things that showed that they cared. However, when we invited them to come and visit the archive, they didn't want to come. Only very few of them ever [did]. We had open days, in the same spirit so that they could see what happened with their contributions. I remember, one man coming and looking at me and looking at the collection and saying, 'Oh it's all much smaller than I imagined.' [Laughing] You know, it's always a big disappointment. So, it's a fantasy for them really.

And, of course, they get their feedback [about use of the material] in other ways, for example in television plays, or films, or books. In those directives I was completely responsible for, I tried to send them information about how things were being used and who was using them, and links to books that were coming out, so that if people wanted to follow it up, they could. And that wasn't just about their own material, but about the history of the older Mass Observation material as well. I think a lot of people joined the new project because they'd read Nella Last. They thought of themselves as the present-day Nella Last. If there was an interview on *Woman's Hour*, we'd get a lot of volunteers writing in and they quite liked this slightly observer-ish position. I remember once, I gave a talk in Bolton, which was a bit like going back to Mass Observation in the 1930s, in fact, it was weird because everything was different from what I imagined, because I'd only had a vision of Bolton in 1937 [from the old papers]. But, there was somebody in the audience, who wrote to me afterwards, and said, I'm number 432 or whatever, 'I was at the back of that hall, Sheridan. You didn't do too badly'. I realized that [Observers are] everywhere! And I used to say that to students as well, when you're talking about the people you're reading, be respectful, because they might be listening or somebody who also writes might be listening. Don't objectify them. It's this whole thing about them not being data subjects. They're people all around you, they might be the person you live with; they might be anybody. And you need to be respectful of them, because they share so much.

Publication of Mass Observation material has been an important way to promote the archive and to recruit volunteers to write for the organization. Sheridan reflects on the first publication of M-O material to come out in the 1980s, Nella Last's War, *as well as volumes that she edited or co-edited:*

DS: I helped Richard Broad, who edited *Nella Last's War*, just by being there really. He was originally going to make a drama documentary; he was a film producer – television producer – for what was then Thames Television [independent TV company]. That never happened, but he had a lot of money behind him to develop his idea, and enough to type out Nella's diary, or at least the wartime part of it. And I had a vested interest in getting one of the biggest diaries, and the most unreadable in its original handwriting, typed up. So the choice was quite pragmatic really, because Richard had the money. He came down to Sussex with five electric typewriters, which I had never seen before, set them up in the reading room (we had plenty of room at that time), and we hired part-time typists to type it all out. My role was simply to make sure they all got paid, and to help them, as far as I was able, decipher Nella Last's handwriting. I was able to do a little bit more than they could because I'd come from the North, I'd grown up in Yorkshire. Of course she was Lancashire/Cumbria. And I began to see how it might be possible for me to do something similar.

Then Angus asked if I'd like to do a book with him, and we did *Speak for Yourself*, which was not the title we chose; it was the title that Liz Calder, who was at Jonathan Cape, [chose] – it was Jonathan Cape that published it. She went on to found Bloomsbury. But, I was very touched, because it's very easy for somebody who works in an archive and is a clerk – I was paid as a clerk at that time in 1981 – not to be respected or valued. Angus asking me to work with him was a huge boost to me, and really encouraged me. I have a lot to thank him for. He was a very shy, and difficult person to get on with, but you know, he really rated Mass-Observation, and we put together that book quite quickly. We wanted to call it the Bolton Tortoise, because the very first story in it is about a Mass Observer, an observing Mass Observer, recording a conversation about a man with a tortoise – he had it in his coat. There were some literacy projects called 'Speak for Yourself', so I was not keen on the title but we had to have that title to get published. That was the very first book, and that got a huge amount of publicity, partly I think because Angus was so well-known, [especially for] his book, *People's War*. He was quite a well-known figure, and we got reviews in all the main national newspapers, and on television. That whetted my appetite; it seemed to me that it was part of promoting the archive. Unless we put things in books or films and so on, or television programs, people wouldn't know it was there and most people don't visit archives. I was very aware that visiting an archive was a bit of an élite thing that only some people could do. I felt that one of the strengths of Mass Observation was that it produced books that would be accessible to the people who contributed. You know, *Britain by Mass-Observation* (in 1939) was a book that many people could've bought. It was a Penguin special, and it was cheap.

It was while we were still working on [*Speak for Yourself*], that I decided to have a go myself with Naomi Mitchison's diary, and although Naomi Mitchison didn't really fit with the 'ordinary person' sort of thing – she was relatively well-known and a writer herself – I thought that her diary – and she wrote a huge diary – that her diary would be publishable. So, I got in touch with Livia Gollancz, who was running Gollancz at the time.

She came down to see me, and gave me the green light. Naomi was very happy about that. In fact, the version of the diary that's in the archive is the carbon paper copy. Naomi had the top copy in a drawer in her house in Scotland, which was much easier to read and also wasn't censored. She sometimes took the carbon paper out when she was doing the version for Mass Observation, mainly to protect individual people. I think if they were doing something illegal and she was writing about it, she didn't put it in her version to Mass Observation. [It was] an interesting lesson in having two versions, one for Mass Observation. Research for the book went on for another two or three years. Naomi said that I had to go up and see her. I had to do my research in her house, which of course was where she was living in the war, in Carradale [Scotland]. So I went to this enormous house – with these terribly upper-class socialists. It was terrifying. The first time I went there, I went with Angus, because he was interviewing Naomi for some Scottish poetry thing. The second time, I took my son with me, and he ate nothing because he was a fussy eater. She'd plonk something down and say this is venison crumble or something. 'I'm not eating that mummy?' [he would say]. The third time, I took a woman friend with me, Julia, who is my best friend. And that was the best and the most productive, because she and I could talk about the work in progress. Naomi could be very kind but she was also very prickly, a bit arrogant, and had lived a most amazing life. You couldn't help but respect her. I liked her because she was a socialist and a feminist, but not an easy person to get on with. And the Mull of Kintyre is the most beautiful place. It was interesting being in the same house where the diary had been written – it helped me understand it.

The third book was on *Mass Observation at the Movies*, which I did with a film specialist, Jeffery Richards. Again it was more or less an anthology of file reports and so on. It wasn't really writing – well it was – we wrote the in-between bits. I've always felt that I've never done a monograph of my own writing. It's always been presenting Mass Observation. And then finally, something I'd been putting on hold. I wanted to do a book about women's writing for the archive. It was delayed because I had signed up for an MA in History by then and I had to renegotiate my deadline with the publishers. I returned to it in time for publication in 1990. I really wanted to do [*Wartime Women*], which is why I didn't continue with my academic work beyond the MA. My MA research had not been on Mass Observation. Instead I did an oral history project on women who had been in the British army, in the ATS, of which there's hardly anything in Mass Observation. Then the final book I did from Mass Observation, with Brian Street and

David Bloome, [*Writing Ourselves*] came out in 2000 and that was much more about the new [MO] project.

Mass Observation and its archives present opportunities for researchers and writers across a wide range of disciplines and endeavours.

DS: [Annabella Pollen] looked at the way that different disciplines have used Mass Observation. It was a very useful summary of the way different people have used it.[12] For example, cultural historians, cultural studies [researchers], have done work in this area on subjects like mantel pieces, the detailed descriptions that Mass Observation made of things like people's wall paper or the interiors of their house or their furniture, on and off over the years going right back to the 1930s and right up through the contemporary project where the people themselves, as part of the panel, would send in drawings of their cushions. There was one woman who sent in the most elaborate, detailed drawings of her furniture and paintings on the wall and flowers! All in colour, she did. So, for a visual historian or, you don't have to be a historian, there's really a lot [for] architecture and design. So from that point of view, access to information about how people lived, rather than that they lived. People's sitting rooms, for example, you sometimes go to museums and you see a 1950s sitting room, and everything in it is from the 1950s. But of course people don't live like that; they have things that go back to their grandma, they have modern things, so everyday life is much more of a mixture. So I think that for people who are looking at the lived experience of design and visual imagery, it's been very important, and could go on being important. [Another] topic is health and well-being for medical researchers, medical sociologists, from the point of view of subjectivity: how do people understand what's going on in their bodies? And there's one person [Jill Kirby[13]] who did a study of stress, and that was really interesting, because the concept of stress is historically specific. So, she could do a search for 'stress' but not find it, because they didn't use that word at the time; this is something for linguists, too. You can find out about concepts and when they start to be labelled in particular ways, and the ways in which words get used gradually, at least in written accounts. But that's something else to do with, say, corpus studies, where people will analyse huge amounts of data. The fact that it's now digitized makes it much more, well, completely open to that kind of research. I think it's always going to be useful to political historians because of the subjective aspects of how people change their minds, and what people will say when they're in the privacy of their own homes and writing, may be very different, this is what Harrisson used to say, and I think he's right – there are layers of public views. So, for politicians or for political scientists, then, there's always going to be more.

And because Mass Observation is still collecting, and has been collecting through the pandemic, I think there will be a lot of stuff there that will be very useful. As for women's history, that goes on being important. I think that most of the arts and social studies will find something there. People don't expect it. Part of it is they're being imaginative about how to look. I think it's also useful in the non-academic areas, like for novelists. In fact, a number of novelists do cite Mass Observation as being one of the places they go to find out what kind of films people were watching or what their language was like, and I think that's really interesting. [For example, Sarah Walter's novel, *Nightwatch* set in the Blitz.] I suppose too it can encourage people to write.

Sheridan reflects on how the Archive has evolved since the 1990s and considers challenges confronting the Archive as well as the many opportunities open to the Mass Observation Project and the Archive in the future.

DS: [In the 1990s], we had a regular research seminar, we had an Occasional Paper series, we gave talks, and we had courses relating to it. When we started doing our seminar series, people would plan their research visits on the day of the seminar, and although they weren't all on Mass-Observation, they were on related methodological issues, or wartime issues, people talking about how they used the collection in a way which allowed other people to think about how they could use the collection. The seminars were very popular and very well attended. We set up the Center for Life History Study, Al [Thomson] and I. All that's changed now, but then Sussex has completely changed. You know, a lot of these things are products of their time, aren't they? What people want at the time – they don't necessarily die, they just change. So the archive was much, much more than a public service, you know, sort of an archival resource. It was a place where people met; it had an atmosphere and it was a kind of intellectual place to come. People met each other, and made friends, and shared ideas. But you can't do that at the Keep, you just can't. You know, you're sitting in a room, with people providing you with boxes who may be brilliant on local history of Brighton, but don't know anything about what they're giving you. And unless you know to ask the right questions, and ask to talk to Jessica [Scantlebury] or Fiona [Courage], you'll never get more than that. Fiona used to say to me, quite rightly, that my knowledge of the material needed to be externalized, it had to be made more available. And that's what they've done really, they've put it into catalogues and finding aids. I did worry about the epistemological challenges of having a digitized version, because it does mean that you could, possibly, search, for example, [someone] doing a project on religion in the 1930s, could find a description of a chapel, a

Methodist chapel, in Bolton, in 1937, without knowing anything about how it was created, or about the context, or who wrote it, or why, or anything about Mass-Observation. It puts the responsibility, I think on the students, anyway on the teachers, to help students think about how this document [was] generated.

[Recently, Mass Observation has] been able to do all sorts of projects. For instance, Suzanne [Rose] has developed a project in Lewes Prison, where she's using what we've produced, copies of it, to take to prisoners and to get the prisoners to write. Some of the prisoners are extremely literary, and literate, and some prisoners have struggles. And their writing gets preserved, if they want it. So I think that's one of the directions that Mass Observation can move in, which is perhaps more democratizing, doing one-off projects with specific people – homeless people were one project, the gay community was another, there's a focus on a particular community. Because I think there's always going to be a limit to who you can recruit to just write on a regular basis. And, it's good I think. I mean, for many years, maybe people don't ask this anymore, people would say why don't you recruit people who are more representative. And the answer is, you can try, tell me how to do it. Because it's a very specific thing writing for Mass Observation, with all sorts of ideas about gender, class and power. You can't just make people write about their everyday lives, and if you did, in some way, it wouldn't be very valuable, because they wouldn't be being their own self. Whereas working with schools, or students, and going in all kinds of other directions, you can diversify – if the project has the resources, which is why I think Kirsty [Patrick] and Suzanne are two key, pivotal people, to keep bringing in new material. And why, when I think of the new project, or the Mass Observation Project [as the more recent work is known], it can be more than the panel writing, it's got to be, it always has been. They may not have the continuity which is of course, one of the strengths [of the longitudinal panel]. I mean, one of the strengths of the wartime diaries is that the same people wrote over a long time and part of the research could be looking at how people change. And that's true, too, for the new panel material, you could track somebody, a few people, who started writing in 1981 and carried on to now, and see how they have changed. There are not many other sources of data where you could find that quality, especially not all together. But we may have to sacrifice some of that in order to encourage people to write who might otherwise not write. And then, of course, there's the material generated by the new sort of social networking, social communication, and Twitter, and other people are recording websites and blogs and logs and whatever, Twitter, Instagram. What we should be recording is, not the actual things themselves, but how people feel about them, who's using them.

Since retiring from Sussex, Sheridan continues to work with her community and life stories:

DS: I re-trained as a teacher of English to speakers of other languages, and my whole world now is working with different kinds of life stories: refugees, migrants, asylum seekers and teaching English. Although [because of the pandemic] it's been reduced sometimes to teaching on WhatsApp because that's all my students have. Nevertheless, you know, my world has changed. I work much more in the town [away from the University], with very different kinds of people. It helps me understand a bit about the past, you know, it helps me reflect back. It's still life stories, it's still dealing with people. Although working in an archive is apparently working with pieces of paper, it never was just that for me, it was the people who wrote and the people who came in and used it, that made it what it was really.

Notes

1. Kiernan Connell and Matthew Hilton, 'Stuart Hall and the Birmingham Centre for Contemporary Cultural Studies', *Discover Society* (4 March 2014). https://archive.discoversociety.org/2014/03/04/stuart-hall-and-the-birmingham-centre-for-contemporary-cultural-studies/ (accessed 6 January 2022).
2. Dorothy Sheridan, 'The Mass Observation Archive: A History', *Mass Observation Online*. 2009. http://www.massobservation.amdigital.co.uk/FurtherResources/Essays/TheMassObservationArchiveAHistory (accessed 6 January 2022).
3. Nick Stanley, 'Memories Refracted through Later Experience: The Early Mass Observation Participants' Interviews', unpublished essay (2017), Mass Observation Archive, 1.
4. Quoted in Nick Stanley, 'Memories Refracted through Later Experience: The Early Mass Observation Participants' Interviews,' unpublished essay (2017), Mass Observation Archive, 1.
5. Quoted in Nick Stanley, 'Memories Refracted through Later Experience: The Early Mass Observation Participants' Interviews,' unpublished essay (2017), Mass Observation Archive, 1.
6. Nick Stanley, 'Memories Refracted through Later Experience: The Early Mass Observation Participants' Interviews,' unpublished essay (2017), Mass Observation Archive, 4.
7. Upon reflection after the interview, Stanley shared what he believed connected his early work on Mass-Observation with his subsequent career, 'It is the fascination

with material culture and how people both form it and are shaped themselves by it. This was the thread that I think I was trying to follow in M O with the artistic dimension, and it is an aspect of anthropology that I've remained fascinated by ever since'. Personal communication (email), May 30, 2022.
8   Penelope Summerfield, 'Education and Politics in the British Armed Forces in the Second World War', *International Review of Social History* 26, no. 2 (1981): 133–58.
9   Penny Summerfield, *Women Workers in the Second World War: Production and Patriarchy in Conflict* (London: Routledge, 1989).
10 Gail Braybon and Penny Summerfield, *Out of the Cage: Women's Experiences in the Two World Wars* (London: Pandora, 1987).
11 *Journal of Contemporary History* 20 no. 3 (1985): 439–52.
12 Annabella Pollen, 'Research Methodology in Mass Observation Past and Present: "Scientifically about as valuable as a chimpanzee's tea party at the zoo"'? *History Workshop Journal* 75 (Spring 2013): 213–35.
13 Jill Kirby, 'Working too Hard: Experiences of Worry and Stress in Post-War Britain', in *Stress in Post-War Britain, 1945–85,* ed. M. Jackson (New York: Routledge, 2015), Chapter 4.

Bibliography

Ashplant, Timothy. '"Subjective Cameras": Authorship, Form, and Interpretation of Mass Observation Life Writings'. *The European Journal of Life Writing* (2021) 10: MO16-MO44. https://ejlw.eu/article/view/37404 (accessed 24/1/2022).

Barson, Tanya. 'Time Present and Time Past'. In *Making History: Art and Documentary in Britain from 1929 to Now* [exhibition publication], 9–26. London: Tate Publishing, 2006.

Blackman, Tim. 'Raymond Williams and the New Industrial Trainers: A Critique and a Proposal'. *Oxford Review of Education* (2021): 1–15. DOI: 10.1080/03054985.2021.1997732 (accessed 24/1/2022).

Bloome, David, Dorothy Sheridan and Brian Street. 'Theoretical and Methodological Issues in Researching the Mass-Observation Archive'. *Mass Observation Archive Occasional Paper* No.1 (1993), University of Sussex Special Collections: Mass Observation Archive.

Bolton Museums. 2020. 'A Little Festival of Mantelpieces'. https://www.boltonlams.co.uk/news/article/12/a-little-online-festival-of-mantelpieces (accessed 24/1/2022).

Bytheway, Bill. 'Writing about Age, Birthdays and the Passage of Time'. *Ageing & Society* 29, no. 6 (2009): 883–901.

Calder, Angus. 'Mass-Observation, 1937–1949'. In *Essays on the History of British Sociological Research*, edited by Martin Bulmer, 121–36. Cambridge: Cambridge University Press, 1985.

Calder, Angus. *The People's War: Britain, 1939–45*. London: Jonathan Cape, 1969.

Campsie, Alexandre. 'Mass-Observation, Left Intellectuals and the Politics of Everyday Life'. *The English Historical Review* 131, no. 548 (2016): 92–121. https://doi.org/10.1093/ehr/cew052 (accessed 24/1/2022).

Casey, Emma, *Women, Pleasure and the Gambling Experience*. London: Routledge, 2008.

Casey Emma, Fiona Courage and Nick Hubble, 'Special Section Introduction: Mass Observation as Method'. *Sociological Research Online* 19, no. 3 (2014): 129–35.

Cook, Terry. 'The Archive(s) Is a Foreign Country: Historians, Archivists, and the Changing Archival Landscape'. *The American Archivist* 74, no. 2 (2011): 600–32.

Courage, Fiona. 'Using the Mass Observation Project: A Case Study in the Practice of Reusing Data'. *Przegląd Socjologii Jakościowej* XV, no. 1 (2019): 32–40.

Cross, Gary, ed. *Worktowners at Blackpool: Mass-Observation and Popular Leisure in the 1930s*. London: Routledge, 1990.

Curzon, Lucy. *Mass-Observation and Visual Culture: Depicting Everyday Lives in Britain*. London: Routledge, 2017.

De Certeau, Michel (with Dominique Julia and Jacques Revel) in 'The Beauty of the Dead: Nisard'. In *Heterologies: Discourse of the Other*, translated by Brian Massumi, 119–36. Minneapolis: University of Minnesota Press, 1986.

Edwards, Alison and Keith Wyncoll. *'The Crystal Palace Is on Fire!' Memories of the 30th November 1936*. London: The Crystal Palace Foundation, 1986.

Foster, Victoria. 'The Return of the Surreal: Towards a Poetic and Playful Sociology'. *Qualitative Sociology Review*, 15, no. 1 (2019): 148–64.

Gascoyne, David. *Journal 1936–37, Death of an Explorer, Léon Chestov*. London: Enitharmon Press, 1980.

Hall, David. *Work Town: The Astonishing Story of the 1930s Project That Launched Mass-Observation*. London: Orion, 2016.

Harrisson, Tom. *Britain Revisited*. London: Gollancz, 1961.

Harrisson, Tom. 'The Future of Sociology'. *Pilot Papers* II, no. 1 (1947): 10–25.

Harrisson, Tom. *Living through the Blitz*. London: Penguin, 1978.

Harrisson, Tom. 'Preface'. 1943. In *The Pub and the People*, 7–14. Reprint. London: Faber and Faber, 2009.

Harrisson, Tom. 'Preface'. In *The Pub and the People*, 5–12, 2nd edition. Welwyn Garden City: Seven Dials Press, 1970.

Harrisson, Tom. 'What Is Public Opinion?' *Political Quarterly* 11 (1940): 368–83.

Harrisson, Tom, Humphrey Jennings and Charles Madge, 'Anthropology at Home'. *New Statesman and Nation* (30 January 1937): 155.

Hinton, James. *The Mass Observers: A History, 1937–1949*. Oxford: Oxford University Press 2013.

Hoshino, Masashi. 'Humphrey Jennings's "Film Fables": Democracy and Image in the Silent Village'. *Modernist Cultures* 15, no. 2 (2020): 133–54.

Hubble, Nick. *Mass Observation and Everyday Life: Culture, History, Theory*, 2nd edition. Basingstoke: Palgrave Macmillan, 2010.

Hubble, Nick. 'Review of Mass Observation Online'. *Reviews in History* 969 (2010a): n. pag. https://www.history.ac.uk/reviews/review/969 (accessed 24/1/2022).

Hubble, Nick, Jennie Taylor and Philip Tew, eds. *Growing Old with the Welfare State: Eight British Lives*. London: Bloomsbury Academic, 2019.

Hume, David. *Treatise on Human Nature* (edition edited by L. A. Seby-Bigge). Oxford: Clarendon Press, 1896.

Hurdley, Rachel. 'Focal Points: Framing Material Culture and Visual Data'. *Qualitative Research* 7, no. 3 (2007): 355–74. https://doi.org/10.1177/1468794107078516 (accessed 24/1/2022).

Hurdley, Rachel. *Home, Materiality, Memory and Belonging: Keeping Culture*. Basingstoke: Palgrave Macmillan, 2013.

Hurdley, Rachel. 'Synthetic Sociology and the "Long Workshop": How Mass Observation Ruined Meta-methodology'. *Sociological Research Online* 19, no. 3 (2014):177–202.

Inglis, David. 'What Is Worth Defending in Sociology Today? Presentism, Historical Vision and the Uses of Sociology'. *Cultural Sociology* 8, no. 1 (2014): 99–118.

Jackson, Julian. *France: The Dark Years, 1940–1944*. Oxford: OUP, 2001.

Jardine, Boris. 'Mass-Observation, Surrealist Sociology, and the Bathos of Paperwork'. *History of the Human Sciences* 31, no. 5 (2018): 52–79. doi:10.1177/0952695118818990 (accessed 24/1/2022).

Jeffery, Tom [no title], *Mass Observation Occasional Papers* 1978: n. pag. University of Sussex Special Collections: Mass Observation Archive. http://www.massobs.org.uk/images/occasional_papers/10_jeffery.pdf (accessed 24/1/2022).

Jennings, Humphrey. *Spare Time*. UK: GPO Film Unit, 1939. https://player.bfi.org.uk/free/film/watch-spare-time-1939-online (accessed 24/1/2022).

Kafka, Ben. 'Paperwork: The State of the Discipline'. *Book History* 12 (2009): 340–53.

Kirby, Jill. 'Working Too Hard: Experiences of Worry and Stress in Post-War Britain'. In *Stress in Post-War Britain, 1945–85*, edited by M. Jackson. New York: Routledge, 2015, Chapter 4.

Kramer, Anne-Marie. 'The Observers and the Observed: The "Dual Vision" of the Mass Observation Project'. *Sociological Research Online* 19, no. 3 (2014): 226–36.

Kushner, Tony. *We Europeans? Mass-Observation, Race and British Identity in the Twentieth Century*. Aldershot: Ashgate, 2004.

Kynaston, David. *Austerity Britain 1945–1951 (Tales of a New Jerusalem)*. London: Bloomsbury, 2008.

Langhamer, Claire. '"Who the Hell Are Ordinary People?" Ordinariness as a Category of Historical Analysis'. *Transactions of the Royal Historical Society* 28 (2018): 175–95.

Last, Nella, in *Nella Last in the 1950s*, edited by Patricia and Robert Malcolmson. London: Profile Books, 2010.

Last, Nella, in *Nella Last's Peace: The Post-War Diaries of Housewife, 49*, edited by Patricia and Robert Malcolmson. London: Profile Books, 2008.

Last, Nella, in *Nella Last's War: The Second World War Diaries of Housewife, 49*, edited by Richard Broad and Suzie Fleming. London: Profile Books, 2006.

Lewis, C. Day, ed. *The Mind in Chains: Socialism and the Cultural Revolution*. London: Frederick Muller, 1937.

Madge, Charles. 'Magic and Materialism'. *Left Review*, no. 3 (1937).

Madge, Charles and Humphrey Jennings, eds. 1937. *May the Twelfth: Mass-Observation Day-Surveys by over Two Hundred Observers*. Reprint. London: Faber and Faber, 2009.

Madge, Charles and Tom Harrisson, eds. 1938. *Mass Observation: First Year's Work*. Reprint. London: Faber and Faber, 2009.

Madge, Charles and Tom Harrisson, *Mass-Observation* [Pamphlet]. London: Frederick Muller, 1937.

Mass Observation. 'Autumn Directive'. University of Sussex Special Collections: Mass Observation Archive, 1983.

Mass Observation. *Home-Front History and Mass-Observation* [pamphlet]. SxMOA32/120/10/1. University of Sussex Special Collections: Mass Observation Archive, n.d.

Mass Observation. 'Mantelpiece Directive'. University of Sussex Special Collections: Mass Observation Archive, 1937.

Mass-Observation. 'Poetic Description and Mass-Observation'. *New Verse*, no. 24 (February–March 1937).

Mass Observation. 'Winter Directive'. University of Sussex Special Collections: Mass Observation Archive, 2019.

Miller, Tyrus. 'Documentary/Modernism: Convergence and Complementarity in the 1930s'. *Modernism/Modernity* 9 (2002): 225–41.

Mills, Charles Wright. *The Sociological Imagination*. Oxford: Oxford University Press, 1959.

Moor, Liz and Emma Uprichard. 'The Materiality of Method: The Case of the Mass Observation Archive'. *Sociological Research Online* 19, no. 3 (2014): 136–46. doi:10.5153/sro.3379 (accessed 24/1/2022).

Moore, Niamh. '(Re)Using Qualitative Data?'. *Sociological Research Online* 12, no. 3 (2007): 1–13.

Pollen, Annebella. 'Research Methodology in Mass Observation, Past and Present: "Scientifically, about as Valuable as a Chimpanzee's Tea Party at the Zoo"?' *History Workshop Journal* 75 (2013): 213–35.

Purbrick, Louise. *The Wedding Present: Domestic Life beyond Consumption*. London: Routledge, 2007.

Robinson, Lucy. 'Collaboration in, Collaboration out: The Eighties in the Age of Digital Reproduction'. *Cultural and Social History* 13, no. 3 (2016): 403–23.

Savage, Mike. 'Changing Social Class Identities in Post-War Britain: Perspectives from Mass-Observation'. *Sociological Research Online* 12, no. 3 (2007): 14–26.

Savage, Mike. 'Revisiting Classic Qualitative Studies'. *Historical Social Research/Historische Sozialforschung* 30, no. 1 (2005): 118–39.

Sheridan, Dorothy. 'Appendix'. In *The Pub and the People*, 2nd edition, 351–4. London: Cresset, 1987.

Sheridan, Dorothy. 'Damned Anecdotes and Dangerous Confabulations: Mass-Observation as Life History'. *Mass-Observation Archive Occasional Paper* No. 7 (1996). University of Sussex Special Collections: Mass Observation Archive.

Sheridan, Dorothy. 'The Mass Observation Archive: A History'. *Mass Observation Online*. 2009. http://www.massobservation.amdigital.co.uk/FurtherResources/Essays/TheMassObservationArchiveAHistory (accessed 6/1/2022).

Sheridan, Dorothy. 'Reviewing Mass-Observation: The Archive and Its Researchers Thirty Years On'. *Forum Qualitative Sozialforschung/Forum: Qualitative Social Research* 1, no. 3 (2000): Art. 26.

Sheridan, Dorothy and Angus Calder, eds. *Speak for Yourself: A Mass-Observation Anthology 1937–1949*. London: Jonathan Cape, 1985.

Slee, Richard. 'Mantelpiece Observations' (Ceramics Exhibition), 2020.

Spender, Humphrey. *Lensman: Photographs 1932–52*. London: Chatto and Windus, 1987.

Stanley, Liz. 'Archaeology of a Mass Observation Project'. In *Manchester Sociology Occasional Papers* No. 27. Manchester: Department of Sociology, University of Manchester, 1990.

Stanley, Liz. 'Mass-Observation's Fieldwork Methods'. In *Handbook of Ethnography*, edited by Paul Atkinson, Amanda Coffey, Sara Delamont and John Lofland, 92–108. London: Sage, 2001.

Steedman, Carolyn. *Dust: The Archive and Cultural History*. Manchester: Manchester University Press, 2001.

Steele, Tom. 'Cultural Studies and Radical Popular Education: Resources of Hope'. *European Journal of Cultural Studies* 23, no. 6 (2020): 915–31. doi:10.1177/1367549420957333 (accessed 24/1/2022).

Stewart, Michael. 'Mysteries Reside in the Humblest, Everyday Things: Collaborative Anthropology in the Digital Age'. *Social Anthropology/Anthropologie Sociale* 21 (2013): 305–21. https://doi.org/10.1111/1469-8676.12041 (accessed 24/1/2022).

Summerfield, Penelope. 'Education and Politics in the British Armed Forces in the Second World War'. *International Review of Social History* 26, no. 2 (1981): 133–58.

Summerfield, Penny. 'Mass-Observation: Social Research or Social Movement?'. *Journal of Contemporary History* 20, no. 3 (1985): 439–52. http://www.jstor.org/stable/260353 (accessed 24/1/2022).

Summerfield, Penny. *Women Workers in the Second World War: Production and Patriarchy in Conflict*. London: Routledge, 1989.

Summerfield, Penny and Gail Braybon. *Out of the Cage: Women's Experiences in Two World War*. London: Pandora, 1987.

Taylor, Jennie and Simon Prince. 'Temporalities, Ritual, and Drinking in Mass Observation's Worktown'. *The Historical Journal* 64, no. 4 (2021): 1083–104.

Tolstoy, Leo. 1869. *War and Peace*, translated by Anthony Briggs. Harmondsworth: Penguin, 2007.

Toogood, Mark. 'Modern Observations: New Ornithology and the Science of Ourselves, 1920–1940'. *Journal of Historical Geography* 37, no. 3 (2011): 348–57.

Trevelyan, Julian. 1957. *Indigo Days*, 2nd edition. London: Scolar Press, 1996.

Williams, Raymond. 'The Common Good'. In *Border Country: Raymond Williams in Adult Education*, edited by John McIlroy and Sallie Westwood, 226–31. Leicester: National Institute of Adult Continuing Education, 1993.

Withers, Charles and Diarmid Finnegan. 'Natural History Societies, Fieldwork and Local Knowledge in Nineteenth-century Scotland: Towards a Historical Geography of Civic Science'. *Cultural Geographies* 10, no. 3 (2003): 334–53.

Wood, Victoria. *Housewife, 49*, [Film] Dir. Gavin Millar. UK: ITV, 10 December 2006.

Wright, Rebecca. 'Typewriting Mass Observation Online: Media Imprints on the Digital Archive'. *History Workshop Journal* 87 (Spring 2019): 118–38. https://doi.org/10.1093/hwj/dbz005 (accessed 24/1/2022).

Index

Abdication Crisis 3, 11, 34, 45
Abyssinia 3, 8–9, 35
Adams, Mary 115
Addison, Paul xii, 121
advertising 3, 10, 20, 26 n.14, 39, 54
ageing 84
air raids 37–8
amateurism 31, 46, 52, 83–4, 103–4, 124
Among You Taking Notes: The Wartime Diaries of Naomi Mitchison 100, 129
anthropology 8–10, 12, 25 n.10, 31, 34, 39, 41–3, 48–9, 53, 58, 64–5, 70, 106, 124, 134 n.7
anthropology of ourselves 1, 8, 34, 70
antisemitism 56, 63, 115
archives 5, 71–5, 79, 99–100, 102, 109–10, 121–3, 126–9, 132
Army Education 109–11
art 8, 22, 32, 39–40, 42–4, 49–50, 55, 83–7, 105
Ashington Group 83–4, 103
Asmat, the 106
atavism 8–9, 35
Austria 3, 48

Baldamus, Gi 101
Balfour, Henry 62
Barlow, Penelope 91
Bell, Graham 86–7
Bergson, Henri 40
Beveridge Report 110
bias 15, 46, 48, 53, 116
Big Data 83
Birmingham City University 105
Birmingham University. *See* University of Birmingham
Black Lives Matter (BLM) 2
Blackpool 25 n.5, 56, 89–90
Bloome, David 131
Bolton x, 25 n.5, 53, 56, 68 n.4, 76–9, 86–7, 89–90, 103, 128–9, 133
Bolton Museum 73, 80, 85

Bowley, Arthur 76
Braybon, Gail 112
Brexit 1
Briggs, Asa xii, 107, 118, 121–2, 124
Britain by Mass-Observation x, 129
British Association for the Advancement of Science 62
British Broadcasting Corporation (BBC) 23–4, 120
British Museum 106
British Union of Fascists (BUF) 3
Broad, Richard 128–9
Bytheway, Bill 84

Cable Street Riot 3
Calder, Angus xii, 99, 102, 121–2, 124, 129–30
Calder, Liz 129
Cambridge University 106
Campaign for Nuclear Disarmament (CND) 118
Cantril, Hadley 57
Carpentier, Nico 24
Casey, Emma 84, 91
Center for Life History (Sussex) 132
Centre for Contemporary Cultural Studies (CCCS) 101
Chamberlain, Neville 82
Chapman, Dennis 102–4
Chicago School of Sociology 76
Churchill, Winston 109–10
civil society 2, 5, 8
civilization 8, 35, 92
class 36, 38, 46, 53, 58, 63, 83–4, 89–90, 103–4, 124
Coldstream, William 85, 97, 102
conspiracy theories 1–2
Contesting Home Defence: Men, Women and the Home Guard during the Second World War 107
Copernicus, Nicolaus 40
Courage, Fiona 132

Courbet, Gustave 44
Covid-19 2, 80, 99, 132
Croce, Benedetto 40
Cross, Gary 89
Crystal Palace 3, 9
cultural history 100, 114–15, 131
Cultural Studies 4, 70, 89, 91, 101, 131
Curzon, Lucy 87

Daily Mirror x, 91
Darwin, Charles 40–1
Dawson, Graham 125
Democracy 1–2, 8, 11–12, 20, 22, 24, 68 n.6, 90
democratization 4–5, 24, 74–5, 84, 89, 92, 126, 133
digitization 71–4, 91, 116, 122, 131–2
dreams 15, 37, 62
Driberg, Jack Herbert 62
Duchamp, Marcel 43

Eco, Umberto 123
Edinburgh Group of Psychical Anthropologists 65
education 38–9, 60, 89–90, 105, 107–9, 111–12, 118–19
Education Act (1870) 38
Edward VIII 3, 11, 34, 45
Egbert, Donald Drew 101
Egypt 36
empiricism 12–14, 31
England, Len xii, 121
entertainment 10, 39
Ethiopia *See* Abyssinia
ethnography 14, 19, 24, 25 n.5, 76, 105–6
eugenics 13
everyday life 4, 8–10, 15, 17, 20, 25 n.10, 45, 57, 60, 63, 67, 70, 82–3, 87, 90, 92, 113–16
experts 39, 47–9, 63

fascism 1–2, 4–5, 9–10, 22, 24, 90
fatalism 37–8
fear 1, 5, 11–12, 37–8
feelings 9–10, 15, 17, 23, 27 n.27, 46, 57
feminism 109, 111–12, 118, 124, 130
film 39, 48–9, 73, 76, 82, 86–7, 130
First World War 112
First Year's Work x, 13, 25 n.5
Folk-Lore Society 64

France 3
Frazer, James 34, 42
Fremlin, Celia 113
Freud, Sigmund 11, 41, 43
Friendly Societies 38

Galileo Galilei 40
Gallery 33 99, 106
gambling 84, 89, 123
gas (poison)13, 37–8, 44
Gascoyne, David 3, 9
George V 34
George VI 18, 45, 87, 90
Germany 3, 6 n.3, 8–9, 35, 67, 68 n.6
Gollancz, Livia 129
Gowing, Lawrence 103
Grierson, John 76

habits 9–11, 13, 21, 34, 45, 53–4, 66, 70
Haddon, A.C. 62
Hall, Stuart 101
Harrisson, Tom x, xi, xiii, 1, 3, 7, 12, 15, 25 n.3 and n. 8, 55, 68 n.4, 70, 78–9, 82–6, 92, 99, 103–6, 109–10, 114, 124–5, 127
  in Bolton x, 76–7
  and MO Archive 100, 118–21, 131
Hencher, Gordon 23–4
Hinton, James 3, 70, 115
Histories of the Self: Personal Narratives and Historical Practice 107
history 75, 107–9, 111–15
Hoggart, Richard 101
Hood, Walter 87, 91
Hoshino, Masashi 74
Hubble, Nick 70, 72, 84
humanism 13–14
Hume, David 13–15
Hunter, Guy 33
Huxley, Julian 13, 31, 41, 67

images 16–17, 27 n.33, 39, 49–50, 71–2, 77, 80, 87, 89
imagination 16–17, 49–50, 74
Imperial War Museum 121
Industrial Welfare Society 66
industrialization 36, 38–40, 42, 45
Inglis, David 75
Institute of Social Research 64
Institute of Sociology 64

Index

internet 2, 23–4
interpretation 19, 47–8, 71, 84, 87
Italy 3, 8–9

Jackson, Julian 3
Jarrow March 3
Jennings, Humphrey x, 19, 33, 71, 76, 87
Jolly, Margaretta 113
Joyce, T.A. 62

Keep, The (Sussex) 71–2, 79, 132
Keith, Sir Arthur 62
Keynes, John Maynard x
Kipling, Rudyard 121
Kirby, Jill 131
Kushner, Tony 115
Kynaston, David 85

Langhamer, Claire 27 n.27, 115
Last, Nella 85, 128–9
Left Book Club 109
Left Review 8, 55
leisure 56, 59, 76, 89
Lever, William 76
Leverhulme Trust 105, 121–2, 126
life writing 125, 134
literacy 3, 10, 38–9, 124, 129
Living through the Blitz xiii, 82, 120, 125
London 8, 33, 49, 53, 56, 64, 86, 102, 108, 121, 127

Madge, Charles x–xii, 1, 3, 4, 7, 11, 12, 17–19, 22, 25 n. 3 and n.8, 55, 76, 78, 91, 99, 101–4
magic 11–12, 22, 36–7, 42–3, 62
'Magic and Materialism' 12
Malinowski, Bronislaw 13, 62, 101
Manchester 56, 76, 87, 100, 107
mantelpieces 18, 21, 49, 51, 80–1, 88, 131
Marett, Robert Ranulf 62
Marienthal (Austria) 49, 68 n.4
Marx, Karl 41
Marxism 12, 119
mass media 2–3, 5, 10, 11, 20, 24, 92
Mass Observation 1, 3–5, 25 n.8, 34, 44–5, 47–9, 51–5, 58, 62, 67, 75–6, 78, 84–5, 90, 92, 99, 101, 103–4, 114, 121–4, 132–3

archive xii, 5, 24, 24 n.2, 70–4, 79–80, 82, 99–100, 102, 104, 109–14, 118–23, 125–8
as counter public sphere 8, 11, 18, 23, 52
criticism of 5, 22–3, 33, 47, 114–15, 123–5
Day Surveys x, 18, 31, 46, 88
Diaries x, xii, 78, 82, 113, 115–16, 133
digitization of 71–4
Directives x, 4, 70, 79–80, 82, 84, 88, 90, 113, 117, 126
as emergent project 4, 7–13, 20
File Reports 84, 113, 120
financing of 54
influence of 23–4, 69–71, 89, 92, 100
method 13–15, 18–21, 31–2, 44–5, 47–8, 52–3, 70–1, 84–7, 89–92, 102, 124, 126, 133
museums 48, 82, 85
poetics of 18–19
representativeness of 51, 54, 116, 124, 133
and science 12–14, 18, 21–2
and social consciousness 20–2, 32
topics of inquiry 58–63
use of 5, 69–70, 72–5, 79–80, 82–5, 114–17, 124–5, 130–2
visuality of 87
Mass-Observation x, 1–5, 7–8, 13, 22
Mass-Observation at the Movies 130
Mass Observation Project xiii, 3, 5, 70–1, 99–100, 113, 116, 126, 131–3
Mass Observers 1, 4, 8, 11, 18–19, 21, 24, 31, 45–8, 51–4, 56–7, 62–3, 69–70, 75–7, 79–80, 82, 89–91, 99–100, 102, 111, 113, 116, 123, 128–9
anonymity of 48, 57
motivation to write 127
recruitment of 5, 33, 54, 67, 68 n.6, 126–8, 133
subjectivity 15–17, 46
materialism 12, 20, 40
May the Twelfth x, 18–19, 73, 87
Melanesia 76, 92
memory 82, 103–4, 117, 125
#Me Too 2
Middletown (United States) 49, 53, 59, 68 n.4
Miller, Tyrus 87
Mills, Charles Wright 70

Mirror (Gordon Hencher) 23–4
Mitchison, Naomi 100, 129–30
Modern Records Centre (Warwick) 122
Mohr, Chris 23
monarchy 11, 19, 34, 45, 54, 90, 120, 126
morality 12–13, 35, 38, 41
Mosley, Sir Oswald 3
multimodality 85, 92
Museum of Culture and Progress (Agats, West Papua) 106
museums 48, 82, 85, 105–6
Myres, John Linton 62
myth 10–11, 13, 38, 62

National Council for Mental Hygiene 66
National Institute of Industrial Psychology 66
Nazism 4, 20, 68 n.6
Nelson, Geoff 101
New Statesman x, 1, 55
New Verse 8, 55
News Chronicle 8, 55
newspapers 3, 8, 10–11, 18, 20, 24, 39, 45, 48, 52, 57, 91
Noakes, Lucy 115
Northern Ireland 101
Novy, Henry 77
Nuer, the 101
Nuffield College 121

Observers. *See* Mass Observers
observing 15–17, 20–1, 34–5, 45–6, 49, 70, 83, 87, 90–1
oral history 100, 111, 113–14, 124–5
ordinariness 17, 70, 82–3, 90, 114–15
Orwell, George 91
Out of the Cage: Women's Experiences in Two World Wars 112–13

Patrick, Kirsty 133
Peake, Harold 62
Peckham Health Centre 65
Pelmanism 49, 68 n.5
Peniston-Bird, Corina 107
People in Production xi
personal narratives 99, 107, 114
philosophy 40, 44
photography 48, 77–80, 85–7
Pocock, David xiii, 80, 100, 126–7
poetics 18, 87

poetry 7, 12–13, 18–19, 50, 76, 86, 91–2
Political and Economic Planning (P.E.P.) 65–6
Pollen, Annabella 131
politics 10, 12–13, 46, 55, 58, 62, 89, 118
Pontypridd 76, 87
Popular Memory Group (Birmingham) 125
presentism 75
Prince, Simon 84–5
prisoners' writing 133
psychology 3, 8–10, 12, 34, 39, 43, 48–9, 57–8, 64–6
public opinion 14–15, 24, 58
public sociology 81, 89
Purbrick, Louise 79

race 46, 54–6, 58
racism 2, 10, 20
Radical Socialism and the Arts 101
radio 2–3, 10, 20, 24, 37, 39, 45, 58
Raine, Kathleen 8, 91
Randall, Vicky 104
realism 37, 40, 44, 86–7
reflexivity 4, 7, 8, 77, 84–5
religion 36, 38–9, 46, 55, 57–8, 62
Rhineland 3
Richards, Audrey 62
Richards, Jeffery 130
Rimbauld, Arthur 42–3
Robinson, Lucy 72, 79
Rose, Mandy 23
Rose, Suzanne 133
Royal Observatory Archive (Herstmonceux) 122–3
Rustin, Michael 115

St. Andrews University Group 64–5
Sarawak Museum xi
Scantlebury, Jessica 132
Science 2–3, 8, 12–13, 18, 20–2, 24, 31, 34–51, 53–5, 63, 124
Scotland 19, 56, 65, 130
Second World War x, 82, 100, 102, 107, 109–10, 112, 117, 120
Seligman, Charles Gabriel 62
Sheffield 76, 87
Sheridan, Dorothy xiii, 5, 70, 72, 79, 83, 91, 99–100, 102, 109, 113, 116, 118–34

Simpson, Wallis 3, 34
Slee, Richard 80-1
social consciousness 4, 20-2, 45, 55
social history 82, 100, 124
social media 2, 24, 133
social psychology 48, 57, 65
Social Psychologists' Group 65
social surveys 49, 59
sociology 5, 8, 31, 34, 48-9, 59, 64, 69-71, 74-7, 79-85, 91-2, 99, 101, 104, 118-19, 122, 124, 126
Solomon Islands 99, 106
Spain 3, 8-9, 35
Spare Time (film) 76, 87
Speak for Yourself 100, 129
Special Collections (Sussex) 100, 121-2, 126
Spender, Humphrey 76-7, 80, 85, 87, 91
Spender, Stephen 76
spiritualism 36, 58
Stanley, Liz 69-70, 87
Stanley, Nick 5, 99, 101-6, 122, 124, 134 n.7
Steedman, Carolyn 74
Steele, Tom 89
Street, Brian 131
subjectivity 9, 14-15, 17, 83-4, 100, 113, 115, 124, 131
Summerfield, Penny 5, 99-100, 107-17, 122, 124-5
superstition 1, 3, 10-14, 20, 22, 35-40, 44, 51, 53
surrealism 10, 85-7, 91-2, 105
Sussex University. *See* University of Sussex

taboo 11, 62
Tarrant, Molly 102
Taylor, Jennie 84-5
technology 2-3, 5, 10, 37, 63, 116
television 2-3, 10, 23-4
Thomson, Alistair 125-6, 132
Thompson, Paul 124-5
Tolstoy, Leo 44, 83
totemism 36, 60, 62
Treatise on Human Nature (Hume) 13-14

Trevelyan, Julian 77, 82-7, 102-3
Tylor, Edward Burnett 41-2

Ukraine 2, 6 n.3 and n.4
United States 1, 49, 53, 64, 67
University of Birmingham xii, 99, 101, 104, 125
University of Lancaster 107, 114
University of Manchester 100, 107
University of Sussex xii, 5, 99-100, 102, 107-8, 112, 118-22, 125-6, 132, 134
University of the Third Age (U3A) 84
University of Westminster 104

Vernon, James 25 n.7
Video Nation 23-4
Vietnam War 118

Walter, Sarah 132
War Factory xi, 113
Wartime Women 100, 130
West Papua 99, 106
Wickham, Michael 77, 86
Wigan 54, 56
Williams, Beryl 108
Williams, Raymond 90
Willcock, Bob xi, xii, 110
Wireless. *See* radio
Wolff, Janet 101
Woolf, Leonard 121
Woolf, Virginia 121
women 84, 100, 108-9, 111-13, 124, 130
Workers' Educational Association (WEA) 83, 90
Women Workers in the Second World War: Production and Patriarchy in Conflict 112
Women's Liberation Movement 109, 111
working class 38, 83-4, 89-90, 124
Worktown Project x, 68 n.4, 76-9, 85, 87, 120
Writing Ourselves 131

Yeo, Stephen 109, 112
Youth 57-8

Ziegler, Philip 126

www.ingramcontent.com/pod-product-compliance
Lightning Source LLC
Chambersburg PA
CBHW050824160426
43192CB00010B/1887